The One Minute Maniac

Jeffrey Book & Garrett Soden

Andrews, McMeel & Parker
A Universal Press Syndicate Affiliate
Kansas City • New York

D1041260

To Denise K. Seider and Nicky Leach,
for enduring countless maniacal minutes.

Acknowledgments: Thanks to George Parker and
Donna Martin for their encouragement and advice,
and to Kathy, David, and Emil Styffe
for working like maniacs to help complete this project.

THE ONE MINUTE MANIAC
Produced for Andrews, McMeel & Parker by

MAD FELLOW PRESS
Los Angeles

The One Minute Maniac copyright © 1987 by Jeffrey Book
and Garrett Soden. All rights reserved. Printed in the
United States of America. No part of this book may be used
or reproduced in any manner without written permission
except in the case of reprints in the context of reviews. For
information write Andrews, McMeel & Parker, a Universal
Press Syndicate Affiliate, 4900 Main Street, Kansas City,
Missouri 64112.

Library of Congress Cataloging in Publication Data

Book, Jeffrey.
    The one minute maniac.

    1. Time management—Anecdotes, facetiae, satire, etc.
I. Soden, Garrett. II. Title. III. Title: 1 minute maniac.
HD69.T54B66 1987   658.4'093   87-914
ISBN 0-8362-1260-6

Copy art manipulations by Garrett Soden.

Typesetting by Cal Press Graphics, El Monte, CA.

Contents

 *The Symbol*

The One Minute Maniac's symbol is intended to remind each of us to take one minute out of our day and look into the faces of the people we manage. And to realize that *they*—with all their faults—are the only thing that stands between us and efficiency.

 *Introduction*

A few years ago, a thin book with a catchy title and a fairy-tale plot became a publishing phenomenon. In this fable a young man seeks—and, incredibly, finds—the Secret to Success, with the help of an unnaturally wise executive who demonstrates that people can be conditioned like lab mice.

This charming story, with its pithy quotes and lists, is inspirational, thought-provoking, and rather silly.

Not to be outdone, we've written our own tale. In our story, another young man finds what he is looking for—although with different results. As in the original, we have restricted the vocabulary to a third-grade level, and hope the reader won't be insulted. Remember, we didn't invent this style. We don't have that kind of nerve.

Enjoyment of The One Minute Maniac does not require familiarity with That Other Book. This book contains its own valuable lesson. (We may have misplaced it, but it's here somewhere.)

Maniacally yours,

Jeffrey Book & Garrett Soden

ONCE there was a serious young man. He was serious because he had a most serious mission—to find the most efficient manager in all the land.

He hoped that when he found this manager, he could be led away from his natural ineptitude toward a magnificent awakening of superhuman power.

He knew it was a longshot.

The young man spent sleepless nights reading the advice of countless gurus, all claiming to show the way to Management Nirvana, until his mind was a fog of dense prose, theories, and buzzwords.

As he devoted all his spare time to the quest, his life became rushed and disorganized. He had to work late to manage his workload. Household tasks went unfinished. His wife and young son hardly saw him. The young man's fellow workers laughed at him, pointing out that despite all his theories, he couldn't organize a desk drawer. Hurt and frustrated, the young man despaired of ever becoming one of America's last heroes – a dynamic, efficient manager.

And yet he continued his search, encountering every kind of manager along the way. He was beginning to see all the various ways in which people manage people. With a clarity common to those of simple mind, he divided them all into two types.

The first type seemed efficient. This kind was always rushing around and yelling. He had a scowl on his face and his employees trembled in his presence. These managers described themselves in very similar terms. "I'm hard-nosed," he was told. "I'm bottom-line-oriented." "I'm God."

They all described their methods for motivating employees in very similar terms. One said, "My employees work till they drop or I stuff their heads in a filing cabinet and kick their butts."

The young man appreciated their discipline, and yet he was disturbed. Who would like a manager that behaved this way? The young man did, after all, want to be liked.

The second type was more sociable. When he arrived at this type's office, a birthday party was usually in progress. Empty pizza boxes and plastic wine glasses littered the desks. The manager could be found in a corner smiling, with beads of sweat on his forehead, glancing nervously at his watch. Occasionally he would say to no one in particular, "Hey, guys, what do you say we do a little work, okay? Just till lunch – then we'll knock off early." No one paid any attention.

These managers also described themselves in similar terms. "I'm people-oriented," he was told. "I'm easy-going." "Oh, gosh, I guess I'm just an old softie."

They seemed to have happy offices, and yet the young man was still not satisfied. How could these managers get anything done? The young man certainly wanted to get things done.

There must be a third kind of manager, he thought, one who combined the best qualities of both. "The perfect manager," the young man reasoned, "would be loved by the very employees he exploited. Surely one exists somewhere." And so his search went on.

One day a gust of wind blew him into a networking seminar where he met a beautiful blonde executive named Glenda. They exchanged business cards.

"Ernest Fellow, Junior Entity," she mused, reading his card. "And what is CanSys?"

"We used to be called Alcanco. Before that, it was Allied Can and Container Corporation," Ernest explained. "A long time ago, the name was Brophy's Neverleak Tins. You may have heard our slogan on TV: *We're People Helping Themselves Help Others Help More People.*"

Glenda smiled but shook her head.

The two went on chatting pleasantly, and eventually Ernest revealed his quest. He told Glenda of his career frustration and his search for the perfect executive role model. "Why, haven't you heard," she asked, "of the One Minute Maniac?"

She went on to tell of this wonderful manager — a wizard who could solve all his problems. This man had been lionized in legend and rumor. People spoke of him in hushed tones.

So great was the power of his wisdom that the First Book of it — thin as it was and costing $15.00 plus tax — was clutched to America's corporate breast like tablets from on high. It passed from one of the faithful to another, an icon of devotion for managers throughout the land. Soon the Second Book came, and then the Third Book.

As the Word became stronger, still more books were delivered unto the true believers; verily, motivational video tapes and board games could not be far behind.

Clearly, there was a nugget of truth here.

He asked Glenda how he could find this man. "Oh, he is not far away," she said. "He can be found at One Maniac Plaza. And although he is very important, he is never busy. Go to him, and you may find what you seek."

Ernest phoned the One Minute Maniac's office and was put through immediately to his public relations staff. They were most helpful. They gave him phone numbers for the Great Man's many retainers, including his personal handler, booking agent, masseur, and pastry chef. They gave him a schedule of the Maniac's coming public appearances and a selection of glowing testimonials from celebrities and moguls. They even told him where to buy the Maniac's new board game, and his motivational video tape, *Beat to Win.*

But for Ernest, this was not enough. He longed to meet the Maniac face to face. Reluctantly, the P.R. people arranged a meeting with someone who could help, a Mr. Stickley at the Maniac's corporate headquarters.

So HE set off for One Maniac Plaza and soon found himself in a beautiful complex of high-rise office buildings, each one shimmering like a jewel in the afternoon sun. In the center stood the tallest one, a great postmodern skyscraper made entirely, like the others, of glistening, emerald-green glass.

"This sure doesn't look like CanSys," Ernest said to himself. Following the directions he'd been given, he headed off down a yellow-carpeted hallway.

The view from Stickley's spacious, twentieth-story suite was one of spectacular breadth. The young man sat down in front of the executive's huge walnut desk and placed his brief case on his knees. He snapped it open with what he hoped was a professional air and took out a notebook.

Mr. Stickley leaned back in his chair. "So, you've come to find out about the One Minute Maniac," he said. "You know, he's quite a guy."

"I'll bet he is!" enthused Ernest. "Does everyone just call him the One Minute Maniac?"

"Either that or the Eternal One of Ultimate Wisdom."

"But why is he called that?"

"Well, Eternal One because we think he'll sell books forever, and—"

"No, no. Why One Minute Maniac?"

"Because he believes good management is simpler than people think and should take less time than it does. He insists on time-efficiency in everything we do—from tying our shoes to firing a lifelong employee. Of course, you shouldn't assume that those two examples require equal amounts of time."

"No, of course not," agreed the young man.

"In fact," Mr. Stickley continued, "firing that employee might well take less time than tying your shoes. If it's done efficiently."

"Oh, I see," said Ernest, not wanting to appear slow-witted.

"We also call him the One Minute Maniac because he can change your life in a minute. He certainly changed mine. When I met the Maniac, I was a mess, and so was my office. Finding anything around here was like looking for a needle in a haystack. And I didn't have the brains to just plow through it all."

"And he changed all that?"

"He sure did. Look around."

The young man looked around. The room *was* tidy. In fact, it was quite bare, lacking anything that might be used for work. There were no files, no typewriter, no mail, no pens, pencils, or paper.

Mr. Stickley noted the boy's amazement. "Now, as you can see, my office is in order and my career has blossomed. As a matter of fact, I'm proud to say I'm outstanding in my field. And it's all because of Minute Scams."

"What are they?" Ernest demanded.

Mr. Stickley's only reply was to give him a well-handled three-by-five card. It read:

*

*Three Words
Good*

*More Words
Bad*

*

"Gosh," marveled Ernest. "What exactly does that mean?"

"We have a rule around here that all goals must be expressed in three words or less."

"Three words?" cried the visitor, incredulous. "But you can't make meaningful plans with a limit like that!"

"That's what I thought. Until I tried it."

"What happened?"

"Well, as I said, this place was a disaster area before. But after talking with his Minuteness, I was inspired. I told all my employees what I have just told you. Naturally, the whole idea was met with a great deal of skepticism. But I forged ahead, setting an example."

"That's what good managers are supposed to do," remarked Ernest.

"What? Hmmm—you might have something there. Anyway, I wrote down my first Scam on a single piece of paper, and instructed them to follow it until it was accomplished."

"What did it say?"

"It said, *Clean This Mess.*"

"That's all?"

"Yep."

"Then what'd you say?"

"Nothing. *There it is,* I said, *plain as day. I can't solve your problems for you.*"

"Now that's delegation!" commented Ernest. "But did everyone understand?"

"They all pretended to, except this new guy. I told him him what the Maniac had said about breaking down a problem into observable and measurable terms."

Mr. Stickley paused as his visitor dutifully wrote down "observable and measurable terms."

"But he still didn't get it, so I all but did his job for him. I said, *Keep the good stuff, toss the junk.*"

"Well, that just sounds like common sense!" his listener exclaimed. "After a detailed and incisive explanation like that, how could he fail?"

"I don't know—but somehow he managed. He made a serious mistake, and I had to let him go."

The young man could hardly believe it. "What happened?" he inquired.

"Little beggar threw away a matchbook from Bubba's Tap Room. Had a lot of sentimental value." A moment of silence was observed while each man reflected upon lost careers and lost matchbooks. Presently the older man spoke.

"And that, in a nutshell, is the Minute Scam."

"I see," said Ernest. "But Mr. Stickley, there must be some situations in which Minute Scamming wouldn't work."

"Like what?"

"Well," said Ernest hesitantly, "say you have three people of equal rank working on the same project. They're good people, but they insist on doing their jobs separately—even though they'd be more efficient if they cooperated. Would you step in? What about trainees? Do they blunder along making mistakes until they figure out how to do their job? What about—"

"You ask too many questions!" snapped the executive. "That won't get you very far in this world, young fellow. Frankly, I have no idea how my staff solves their problems and I don't care, as long as they leave me alone."

"But tell me," Ernest continued, cautiously pressing the point, "how does your staff decide *what* it is to do?"

The executive folded his hands. "I suppose," he replied, a bit more composed, "that you've heard of the 20-80 rule."

"Yes, I have. That's where 80 percent of any company's success comes from only 20 percent of its efforts," volunteered the visitor.

"That's it. Well, we only do the 20 percent that gets results. We skip the rest."

The young man was skeptical. "How, exactly, do you do that?" he said.

"We have a special committee that consults on it."

"It must be a hard-working committee!" the boy exclaimed.

"Not really. Only 20 percent of the committee meets because—obviously—that is all that's necessary. And they only meet 20 percent of the time. And, of course, they only finish 20 percent of their work."

"I think I see what you're driving at," said Ernest. "It's simply a policy of doing only what's needed—and no more."

"Exactly," smiled Stickley, glad to see the stirrings of a newborn Maniac. "Take my day, for example. I get in at noon and start to work by one, take an hour for lunch and then by two I'm done. I've cut out the useless 80 percent of a normal eight-hour day!"

"But doesn't that cut out more than 80 percent of the workday, sir?"

"Very clever! You see, Ernest, that way I'm sure to eliminate the useless part," Mr. Stickley explained patiently.

"But tell me, how do you plan for unexpected situations?"

"I don't PLAN, I SCAM! Haven't you been listening? Good heavens, I still can't keep two halves of a pair of scissors together! I simply *simulate* planning with Minute Scams."

The young man was beginning to understand. "I suppose," he said, "that you have a very good way of rewarding your underlings—err, employees—when they fulfill their Scams. What is it?"

"We call 'em Minute Hypes. You blow some sappy smoke up their chute and they just suck it up. It's great."

"Pardon me, sir, but that sounds a bit...insincere."

Stickley appeared peeved. "Ridiculous. I'm as sincere as the next guy." He looked at his watch. "Look, it's been great talking to you, you're real sharp and I like your suit and all that but I gotta run. If you want to find out more, go bother Woodman down the hall. She'll tell you all about Minute Hypes."

"Thank you very much, Mr. Stickley," said Ernest. "But what about the One Minute Maniac? I'd still like to meet him."

"Oh, you will, don't worry. You're just the type he likes." A knowing smile crossed Stickley's thin lips. "You're perfect."

"Perfect!" echoed the young man, slamming his brief case shut on his tie.

Riding down in the elevator, Ernest condensed what he'd learned about Minute Scams into a few punchy principles.

To Minute Scam, simply:

1. Oversimplify the problem.
2. Oversimplify the solution.
3. Dodge the actual work.
4. Fire anyone who screws up.
5. Take all the credit.

IT WAS now lunchtime, and Ernest decided to spend it in research, to better prepare himself for his next interview. He went to a nearby bookstore and bought every book written by the Maniac. Although he had to spend a small fortune to buy them all, he remained undaunted. He did wonder, however, why they were all so thin and had such large type. It would have been more efficient, he reasoned, for his Minuteness to have written one book, with each subject making up a chapter. But who was he to question the pearls cast before him? It must, he thought, all be part of The Wise One's master plan. He finished the books between bites of his burger, then returned to One Maniac Plaza.

On his way to Ms. Woodman's office he imagined applying what he had learned. Minute Scams seemed so simple. He fantasized about trying the method out on his own subordinates, saying *Clean This Mess* over and over again in his best baritone. Ernest sighed. It would be so much easier if he had subordinates.

Soon he arrived at a big door with a plaque that read "Ms. Woodman." He went in.

"Pardon me," he said to the pert secretary. "Is Ms. Woodman in?"

"Dunno," came the reply. "I can never tell. No one ever comes to see her and she never comes out. Why don't you go in and find out?"

The young man did just that.

Inside, he found a plump woman in her fifties standing with her back to him, gazing out an enormous window. Her body was rigid and motionless — the perfect executive at attention, lost in the world of high-powered decision-making.

Before Ernest could say anything, the alarm on Ms. Woodman's watch beeped. She spun around and began making faces at him — stretching her mouth and eyes wide, scrunching them up, thrusting her tongue in and out. Suddenly she stopped these expressions and began climbing an imaginary ladder. Panting heavily, she spoke to Ernest in a high, squeaky voice.

"Excuse me (huhha, huhha) this is my (huhha, huhha) FitTime (huhha, huhha). Gotta keep (huhha, huhha, HUHHA) fit! (huhha, HUHHA, HUHHA) Onlytakeaminute!"

Abruptly she sat down, picked up the phone, dialed, slammed it down, ripped open her day planner and started scrawling furiously. Ernest was about to speak when she jumped up from her chair, then sat, seized the phone, and started writing again. Ms. Woodman repeated this standing-sitting-dialing-writing sequence faster and faster until she became a frantic blur. Ernest watched her frenzy in amazement, dodging the pens, pencils and paper clips that flew with vicious velocity from her desk.

Finally her watch beeped again, and she collapsed into her chair.

"Keep robust or else you rust, I always say." As she paused to catch her breath she gave Ernest a goofy smile. "Now then—what can I do for you?" The question came so suddenly that it derailed the young man's train of thought.

"What kind of exercises are those?" he blurted out. "I've never seen anything like 'em."

"They're ExecuCises. Real timesavers."

"ExecuCises?"

"Simple idea," Ms. Woodman continued. "You just speed up normal office activities until they become aerobic. You ever do push-ups in a staff meeting?"

"No..."

"Of course not, silly! So why do 'em for exercise? Be better to get faster at what you do at work, doncha think?"

The young man was thunderstruck. "Of course! Why didn't someone think of that before? So that's why you were jumping up and down at your desk. But what about those weird expressions?"

"You mean ExecuSpressions. Keeps my face limber for Minute Hypes and Gripes. You never know when you'll have to go from a grin to a grimace," she said, flashing a grin and a grimace to make her point.

"And the ladder-climbing?"

"Ah, that's my favorite. Up, up, up the corporate ladder!"

Ernest's mind was awash in an ocean of new ideas. How could his poor brain soak it up fast enough? Ms. Woodman's voice broke his trance.

"So. Enough of that. Why are you here? Get to the point, please."

It took Ernest a few moments to remember. "Well, ma'am, my name is Ernest Fellow and I've come to see the One Minute Maniac. I've already visited Mr. Stickley down the hall and he said I should see you before I go on."

"Stickley's just following one of his favorite Minute Scams—'Pass the Buck.'"

"He said you'd tell me about Minute Hypes. Are they the second secret of the One Minute Maniac?"

"Yup," declared Ms. Woodman.

"What's the Maniac like, anyway?"

"Well, he's quite a guy."

"So I've heard," said Ernest.

"Isn't he quite a guy?" she mused.

"I don't know, ma'am, I haven't met him."

"Believe me, he's quite a guy. I changed my whole management style because of him. Before I came here, people said I was a heartless manager. I was known for chopping heads. I admit it—I liked giving people the axe. But after the deadwood was cut, the leftovers would resign. Imagine—the nerve! I could *never* hang on to my employees—until the Maniac showed me how."

"Did it have something to do with Minute Hypes?"

"You bet it did."

"I imagine he showed you how to empathize with your employees. Did he encourage you to spend more time with them? Get to know them, their hopes, their fears, their—"

"Stop talking drivel!" Ms. Woodman interrupted. "I'll do the explaining."

"Sorry," said Ernest.

"Anyway," she continued, "the Maniac told me he wanted me to do well. To do that, he said, I had to know exactly where he stood—and in no uncertain terms. He promised me clear, concise feedback on my job performance. Then he said my earrings were lovely."

She smiled wistfully and fondled the gaudy baubles hanging from her earlobes. "I've worn them ever since."

"He said it might be uncomfortable for us at first. To tell one's truest feelings is always hard. But he said I was very special to him. He put his arm around my shoulder. *If you would get me a cup of coffee,* he told me, *that would be a very good thing.*"

"So I brought it to him. He was pleased—and let me know it right away. *Thank you, Agnes,* he said, *and I must say your taste in shoes is wonderful.* Do you see what he was showing me?"

"The value of career dressing?"

A grimace, for which Ms. Woodman's face was well prepared, appeared. "He was demonstrating," she said sternly, "the power of Minute Hypes."

"Can you give me an example of what you're talking about?" the young man requested.

"I just *gave* you one. The One Minute Maniac takes time to say you're doing well, and reinforces his message by touching."

"Touching? Where does he touch you?"

"None of your business!" Ms. Woodman barked. She added: "But I will tell you he's very good. A very good manager, I mean."

"Well, he doesn't sound like any manager I've ever heard of before. Doesn't that approach take a lot of his time?"

"Not at all. Less than a minute from start to finish."

The youth imagined what it would be like to receive one of the Great One's Minute Hypes. Ms. Woodman's voice interrupted his daydream.

"Let me ask you a question," she said. "When you've done your best at work, what kind of reaction do you get at your company?"

"Not much of anything," Ernest admitted dejectedly.

"Exactly. That's the way it is at most places. But not here. Here, we notice if you're really trying, and take time to tell you. We have a motto that says:

*

*Employees Are
Like Puppies*

*Pat Them
On The Head
And They'll
Lick Your
Boots*

*

"You see," she continued, "we motivate our employees without that vulgar commodity used by most companies."

"What vulgar commodity?"

"Money! That is, anything beyond their meager salaries. Christmas bonuses, profit sharing, raises—we've bagged 'em all. Our employees are conditioned to be content with Minute Hypes. They live for our calculated compliments."

"Oh," said Ernest. He was silent for a moment. "But...well, may I be frank?"

"You be Frank and *I'll* be Ernest," Ms. Woodman giggled.

"Uh, right. Anyway, the one thing that bothers me about all this is that it seems a little...manipulative."

"Manipulative?" the executive fairly shouted. "Why, that's preposterous!" She punched a button on her intercom. "Gladys, come here, please." Turning to Ernest, she continued. "Now, I'll give Gladys a Minute Hype, and you tell me if it's manipulative."

The secretary Ernest had met at the front desk shuffled into the room.

"Oh, Gladys, I need your help on something," Ms. Woodman said, picking up a folder full of invoices. "Straighten these up for me, would you, dear?" She sent the folder sailing across the room, scattering yellow sheets everywhere. Gladys dutifully gathered the invoices while the amazed visitor looked on. When she was done, Ms. Woodman folded her arms and smiled approvingly.

"Fine job, Gladys," she said. "Really super." With this, the executive gave her secretary a hearty clap on the back. Then, smiling intently, Ms. Woodman gazed at Gladys for a brief but meaningful moment. "By the way," she remarked, "that hairstyle makes your face look less pinched. Is it new?"

Gladys perked up. "Why, yes, Ms. Woodman, it's—"

"Thought so. Thanks. Back to work, now!"

Gladys mustered a brave smile and returned to her desk.

"There, you see?" announced the executive. "A Minute Hype is all it takes to keep her happy in her job."

"She did seem a little crestfallen when you cut her off," the young man remarked.

"Nonsense," she said, "Gladys thrives on praise from me, no matter how brief."

Ernest had a flash of insight. "I think I'm beginning to see how a Minute Hype works," he said. "Everyone wants to be loved. In the corporate view, that's an exciting resource to exploit!"

"That's it! Now you're getting it."

As Ernest looked at his notes, he reviewed what he had learned about Minute Hypes.

To Minute Hype your employees, simply:

1. Let them know <u>up front</u> that you're the ultimate judge of their personal value.

2. Reinforce them <u>immediately</u> for correct corporate behavior.

3. Tell them what they did right. If they haven't done anything special, give them a superficial compliment.

4. Take a <u>meaningful moment</u> to let them *"feel"* good about *"feeling"* good.

5. Touch them in a way that makes them *"feel"* even better.

6. Okay, that's enough! Everyone back to work.

"You certainly catch on fast, Ernest," said Ms. Woodman.

"Thank you," Ernest said. "Tell me, how many of these secrets are there, anyway?"

"Three, of course, like all fables. You know—three wishes, three secrets, three little pigs."

"What is the Maniac's third secret?"

Ernest's question was answered by the familiar beeping of Ms. Woodman's watch. "Well," she said, "nice talking with you, but I've got to clean the Velcro on my Minute Planner now. Anyway, you have to stick with the program. Go see Mr. Coward, down the hall. He'll tell you about the third secret."

"Oh. Well, thank you for your time, Ms. Woodman."

"No problem, Ernest—I've had plenty of time since I became a One Minute Maniac," she chuckled.

The young man packed up his things and prepared to leave. As he was about to step through the door, Ms. Woodman called to him.

"Oh, Ernest—I almost forgot."

"Yes?"

"Nice socks."

Ernest was now looking forward more than ever to meeting Mr. Coward and learning the final secret of One Minute Mania.

When he arrived at Mr. Coward's office he saw a large, bearded man with a great mane of brown hair intently studying something on his desk. After a moment he looked up and caught sight of Ernest. "You're Ernest Fellow, aren't you? Come in, come in, don't stand out there in the hallway!" he roared, smiling at his visitor. "I heard you were coming. Have a seat."

The young man entered and made himself comfortable. Before they could begin, however, they were interrupted by the man's secretary. "Excuse me, Mr. Coward," she said pleasantly, "I'm about to make that airline reservation for you. Where did you say the conference is being held?"

Raising his voice the man responded at once.

"I WON'T WASTE MY TIME AND YOURS BY REPEATING MYSELF. IF YOU CAN'T REMEMBER WHAT I SAID, THEN CHECK THE LITERATURE. SOMETIMES YOU HAVE A MIND LIKE A SIEVE. SHAPE UP, BIRD-BRAIN."

The big man was silent for a moment. A tear welled up in the secretary's eye. When it was about to fall, he spoke: "But I love ya, don't ever change, I mean it. Now get outta here, you old so-and-so."

Miraculously, a smile spread across the secretary's face as the tear rolled down and over her lips. Was she laughing or sobbing? Ernest couldn't tell. He was astounded. When she left the room, the manager spoke again.

"See that? Amazing, ain't it? You wouldn't believe it to see her now, but she used to push me around. That's right. I was terrified of her. I used to let all my employees get away with murder because I just didn't have the courage to tell them what was on my mind. But that was before the One Minute Maniac showed me how to do *that.*"

"What *was* that?"

"A Minute Gripe."

"A Minute Gripe?" the young man repeated. "So that's the third secret!"

"You've been counting!" laughed the older man. "Yes, it is. It's a sharp, quick reprimand, to let people know they'd better run with the ball or it's back to the showers. If the Minute Hype is the carrot, the Minute Gripe is the stick."

Ernest was excited that the last of the secrets was nearly his, and yet he was perplexed. "Tell me — what makes it different from regular griping?"

"Oh, it's *much* different," replied the executive. "Much, *much* different. It really is."

"Why?"

"It just is, that's all."

An awkward silence followed. At length, Mr. Coward said, "Now, what can I help you with today, young man?"

"Well, sir," Ernest said, a little uneasily, "I don't mean to be a bother, but I did come to learn about Minute Gripes."

The man was on his feet in a flash. His face turned beet red, and he started shouting.

"YOU WANT TO LEARN ABOUT MINUTE GRIPES? I'LL TEACH YOU ABOUT MINUTE GRIPES! HOW'D YOU LIKE TO GET ONE RIGHT NOW, BUDDY? COME ON. COME ON. LET'S STEP OUTSIDE!"

Ernest gripped the arms of the chair in sheer terror as Mr. Coward loomed threateningly over him. If this is what it felt like to get a Minute Gripe, he didn't like it.

Suddenly, the executive's face became placid. He even smiled. He sat down and began to examine the papers on his desk. As he did, he hummed a little melody, apparently oblivious to his visitor. It was as if the tirade had never occurred.

After quite a while, the young man summoned enough nerve to speak. "Sir?" he said timidly.

Mr. Coward looked up. "Oh, hello, are you still here? What can I do for you?"

He sounded so pleasant that Ernest was able to relax a bit. Perhaps it had all been an act. "I was wondering—was that real, or were you just showing me how it's done?"

"Was what real?"

"Your anger. You sure sounded mad."

"Did I? When? Today?"

"Why, yes, sir. Just a minute ago."

"Oh. Gave you a Minute Gripe, did I? You'll have to pardon me. You see, when I give one, I sort of black out. From the concentration.

"To answer your question, yes, it was real anger. I've spent years perfecting my technique. Sincerity is my trademark," he said with a note of pride in his voice. "I rehearse it daily.

"You might be surprised to learn that when the Maniac first told me about Minute Gripes, I didn't think I'd ever be able to give one. I was too easy-going—how could I focus all that anger, and do it on a moment's notice? But the Maniac told me something that convinced me that I could do it."

"What was that?" said Ernest, more intrigued than ever.

"He told me about a group of people that—although handicapped—are masters at focusing anger. If they could do it, he said, so could I."

"Who was he talking about?" asked Ernest.

"Psychotics."

"I see."

"The Old Man had a saying about it. I had it made into this plaque, which I keep on my desk to serve as a constant reminder of his wisdom."

He handed it to the young man. It read:

*

*Don't Get
Mad*

Get Manic

*

"Anger," he continued, "just hurts people's feelings. If you really want respect, try maniacal rage."

This sounded like a very powerful technique to Ernest. He had to learn more. "Where do you learn something like that?"

"From the masters!" the executive exclaimed. "I, for example, spent my last vacation in a hospital for the criminally insane. Those people wrote the book on assertiveness training."

"That sounds a little dangerous to me!" exclaimed Ernest.

The older man became livid. "WHAT DO YOU MEAN BY THAT, YOU SNIVELING JERK? I DON'T TAKE BACKTALK FROM THE LIKES OF YOU! WHY, I OUGHT TO TEAR YOU LIMB FROM LIMB! I COULD DO IT, TOO, YOU KNOW!!"

Mr. Coward dropped to all fours and began to growl and paw the carpet. "Grrrrrrr. I'm an *animal.* Grrrrrrr," he said.

Ernest, who had drawn his knees to his chest, sat in fear for his life as the apparently berserk executive prowled the office. After a few minutes of this he crawled behind his desk, and Ernest heard no more until a composed Mr. Coward stood up holding a postage stamp he had found on the floor. He looked up and saw Ernest.

"Hello, again! How are you?" he said.

Ernest was beginning to like this moody executive, despite his outbursts. "I think I see how Minute Gripes differ from run-of-the-mill reprimands. If an employee thinks his bad behavior will drive you off the deep end, then he'll toe the line."

"That's the ticket!" smiled the big man, "I think of it as a deep emotional commitment that my employees and I make to each other. And," the old man reminded him, "you must remember that a Minute Gripe isn't all nastiness."

"That's right!" recalled the young man. "After you bawled out your secretary, you said you still liked her. Why'd you do that?"

"It's the bait that keeps 'em hanging on. See, if I just Griped all the time, what would happen?"

"Eventually everybody would quit."

"Right you are, m' boy. Now, if I Griped and yet *always* came back with some lovey-dovey mush, what would happen?"

"No one would pay attention to the Gripe!" Ernest replied enthusiastically.

"Right again! So, here's what I do." Mr. Coward turned to the personal computer on his desk, tapped in a few keystrokes, and peered at the screen. "This week," he said, "I give the mushy part with 37.5 percent of my Gripes. It changes every week—I wouldn't want it to seem calculated!"

"Of course not!" Ernest agreed. "That's thoughtful of you."

"I'm not sure these twits appreciate it." Mr. Coward folded his hands in front of him. "Anyway, that's the story of the Minute Gripe," he said with a smile.

"It all makes perfect sense!" declared Ernest.

"Of course it does," replied his host.

"As far as it goes."

"Why, what do you mean, young man?"

"Well," said the visitor, "what if there's a big problem but you can't find out who's really responsible? Gripe everybody? Or nobody? What do you do if the boss's son works under you, and he is totally incompetent—Gripe all the time, or never?"

"Incompetence," he snorted, "is a state of mind. It never stops anyone here. I can see you're the kind who can't leave well enough alone."

"But what if the situation is more complex?" Ernest persisted. "Say, for example, an employee who is a member of an ethnic minority has performed poorly and you've Minute Griped him accordingly. Then you discover he was actually framed by jealous coworkers who made him look bad. And now his productivity has fallen because he is depressed about being framed. In addition, the coworkers—"

"Those problems," Mr. Coward broke in, "have very simple solutions. But," he smiled, looking at his watch, "I can't answer them now. I'm due to fly off the handle again in 10 minutes. Let's see..." he squinted at the computer screen, "...yeah, Erdman in Marketing's gonna get it." He extended his hand to Ernest. "Sorry. Gotta go. Come again. By the way—like your tie!"

Although his final few questions went unanswered, Ernest still felt he had received a wealth of information. He put away his notes, said goodbye, and hurried home to Norma and little Tommy.

While driving home he went over in his mind the technique of the Minute Gripe:

1. Let people know you've got an insanely short fuse.

2. When they tick you off, blow them away with a sudden burst of <u>maniacal rage.</u>

3. Give them a chance to *"feel"* bad about *"feeling"* bad.

4. Make sure they know it's not *them* you detest, but their behavior—although you can't separate the two.

5. Terrify them with an abrupt emotional reversal by ending with a flash of <u>superficial warmth.</u>

6. Cultivate this love/hate pattern to keep them wondering which end is up.

AT HOME that night over dinner, at Ernest's suggestion, they all discussed the Maniac's methods.

"You know, hon," said Ernest, his mouth full of meatloaf, "this Maniac stuff is really beginning to make sense to me. It's not just pie-in-the-sky. I think if I apply it, I could make a real impression at work. Get a promotion, maybe. Maybe get a raise and make enough so we could be a two-microwave family!"

Norma looked up. "That's nice, dear. I'm glad you're excited. But honey, I really don't need a second microwave."

"No? But didn't you say we all had to wait for the peas to get done before you put in the rolls?"

"Well, sure, but that's only a matter of a few minutes—"

"Norma, that's the point! A few minutes here, a few minutes there, pretty soon we're wasting time right and left. That's what the Maniac's philosophy is all about! Everyone can be more efficient—in dealing with employees, in dealing with loved ones, even in cooking peas and rolls, for cripe's sake!"

"All right, Ernest," said Norma, trying to smooth his ruffled feathers. "I admit we could do things a little more efficiently. I could use a promotion at my job, too."

They cleared and washed the dishes together, Ernest trying to examine each step for wasted motion. That night he fell asleep knowing that tomorrow was a big day. It was the day he would finally meet the Maniac.

WHEN morning came, Ernest could barely contain his excitement. He wasted no time getting to One Maniac Plaza.

Following the directions he'd been given, Ernest arrived at the Great Man's regal, spacious office suite. He looked around the outer office, noticing a large digital wall clock that displayed the time to the hundredths of a second, and admiring the handsome tapestries and sleek modern sculpture. Suddenly, one of the sculptures spoke.

"His Maniacal Highness has been wondering how long it would take you to arrive," said the sculpture. Looking at it closely, Winston realized it wasn't an art object but a robot, with a shiny cylindrical body on wheels. As it spoke, the robot moved its metal arms and blinked its array of lights.

"You mean," said the amazed lad, "he's known all along that I was here? And that I wanted to see him?"

"Of course," said the robot. "The Maniac knows all. And it's not just that he has video cameras everywhere. You see, he has extraordinary powers of perception."

From everything that he had seen, Ernest did believe that the Maniac was someone special – quite a guy, indeed. But he was only a man, and Ernest was a bit suspicious of the adulation heaped upon him. After all, the young man hadn't been born yesterday. He had heard of cults.

"Hasn't the Maniac ever been wrong about anything?" he asked.

"Oh, sure," replied the robot.

This surprised the visitor, but he thought now he must be on to something. "Ah," he said, "what was it?"

"It happened when he published his last book— *The One Minute Presidential Adviser*. For a moment he thought he'd gone too far. But when it sold millions, and became required reading at the White House, he knew he'd been right all along."

"So his mistake was. . .that he thought he made a mistake? Was that it?"

"Yes, that was it. And he had such a sense of humor about it! He'd chuckle and say, *Imagine, me making a mistake! Ha, Ha!*"

The robot laughed heartily, and Ernest joined in. Still, he wondered if the One Minute Maniac could live up to his legend. Soon he would find out.

"When may I see the Maniac?" asked Ernest.

"Unfortunately, the Maniac won't be able to meet with you. He sends his regrets. But I've been programmed to answer your every question."

"But I came to see the Maniac!" cried the visitor.

"I'm sorry, that won't be possible," intoned the robot.

"I don't believe you!" Ernest exclaimed. He darted around the robot and opened the massive polished doors to the inner office. There he discovered a neatly dressed man sitting calmly at a vast slab of a desk.

"Pay no attention to that man behind the desk!" squawked the robot.

"No, no, it's all right, Ronnie," replied the man, rising from his chair. "I'll see this fellow. Thank you, Ronnie. That'll be all."

The robot wheeled around, and was gone. Ernest, by this time, was completely befuddled. "I'm Ernest Fellow. I'm here to meet the One Minute Maniac."

The man fixed Ernest in a gaze that was piercing yet sympathetic. "I'm the Maniac," he said. "It's a pleasure to meet you, Ernest. Please have a seat."

After they were both comfortable, he continued. "Sorry about Ronnie. I guess you didn't expect to be met by a robot. I use him to avoid VisitTime. He's programed to say everything I would have said. You would have been satisfied, and I would have gotten in some GolfTime. But no matter."

So this was the One Minute Maniac. On first glance, the man was not especially impressive. He was of average height and build, with thinning hair and a slight bulge at the waistline. His blue suit was neat, but unremarkable. His only jewelry was a multifunction digital watch. The One Minute Maniac, Master of Minutedom and Czar of Time Efficiency, was a very ordinary-looking middle-aged man.

The Maniac leaned back. He had a reassuring yet forceful manner, Ernest thought. Ernest had felt nervous about meeting His Minuteness; now he found himself dropping his guard. The Master smiled at him.

"Relax," he said soothingly. "What's on your mind?"

"Pardon me, sir, but you—I mean, you're—that is—"

"Not what you expected?" said the Maniac, finishing Ernest's thought. "I know. People make me out to be a wizard, as if I went around waving a magic wand. Truth is, I'm just an ordinary guy, telling people things they already know. Sure, I make millions from it, but that's not the point. I just want to share my wisdom with the masses."

The Maniac studied Ernest's face closely. He got up and walked to the front of the desk, leaning casually against it. He looked directly into Ernest's eyes as he spoke.

"Tell me," he said, "what do you think of the system so far?"

"I think it's...fabulous. I've heard from Mr. Stickley about your Minute Scams, from Ms. Woodman about Minute Hypes, and from Mr. Coward about Minute Gripes. And I admit, they all seem to work."

Ernest paused, smiling up at the Master, but the Maniac's scrutiny remained unbroken. Ernest went on.

"But still...every once in a while I have my doubts."

The older man laughed softly, as if he had heard what he had been waiting for. He put his hand on the young man's shoulder. "Let me tell you a little story," he said. Ernest suddenly felt enthralled by the charisma of this compelling mentor.

"You know, Ernest," the Maniac began, "I was once in your shoes. Years ago, when I first started out, I met a One Minute Maniac. Oh, that's not what he called himself. That's my own little touch. Anyway, it was like being struck by lightning! I immediately became a believer.

"When I returned to my office, I told all my employees about this brilliant man and his wonderful way of working. Some of them laughed in my face and quit. The ones that were left, well, I set to work on them. I'd take a minute to plan Scams, a minute to Hype them and a minute to Gripe at them. But I didn't have the right stuff to make it stick. I overheard employees say I was the most shallow, insincere man they had ever worked for. Needless to say, I was shocked at their arrogance. I pay people to work, not to gossip. At any rate, I, too, lost my faith. I went to my mentor and asked him for help. He didn't say a thing. He just took this card from his desk and gave it to me."

The Maniac showed Ernest the very same card, now dog-eared and worn. It read:

*

*I Have
All The Answers*

*You Have
None Of The Answers*

*

"I've kept it ever since. Whenever I start to falter, I just look at this card. Now, I suggest you do the same."

He handed it to the starstruck young man, saying, "Keep it. It was given as a gift to me many years ago, and so it's only right that I pass it on to you."

Ernest's eyes became teary. His heart was in his throat, and words failed him. "I...I don't know what to say," he managed. "Thank you."

Suddenly they were interrupted by a knock at the door. "Come in," barked the OMM. Ernest was amazed at the Maniac's instant transformation from a kind and sensitive mentor to a tough-sounding manager. In walked a quivering figure of a man.

"What is it, Cromwell?" the Boss said.

"Well, sir, I need more guidance."

"Same problem again? Get out of here, and stop wasting my time. If I've done this once for you, I've done it a hundred times! My God, what do you think the weekly meetings are for? When will you learn to stand on your own two feet, you spineless nincompoop?"

"But, uh, I am standing, sir."

"Oh, all right—but pay attention this time, Cromwell."

"Thank you, sir. Oh, thank you! Please go on!"

The Old Man rose slowly from his desk, trembling with anger, his face red and his fists clenched. "Your interruptions," he began slowly, "are symptomatic of your unwillingness to face your own problems. For weeks I've been listening to you complain, and I'm telling you that *you'd better make a few decisions around here for yourself. That's what you were hired for!*"

As he spoke, his voice grew louder, until the room shook with his bellowing.

"AND IF YOU DON'T HAVE WHAT IT TAKES TO MAKE THESE CRUCIAL EXECUTIVE-LEVEL DECISIONS THEN PERHAPS YOU'D BETTER LEAVE THIS CORPORATION AND GO WORK FOR A LIVING."

Eyes wide, the young man sat in terror. He had never seen anyone whip himself into such a frenzy so quickly—not even Mr. Coward could match this performance. And, incredibly, Cromwell was no longer the diminutive soul who had entered the office moments before. He, too, began to shake with rage. Suddenly, Cromwell's shrill voice burst forth:

"AND IF YOU DON'T HAVE WHAT IT TAKES TO MAKE THESE CRUCIAL EXECUTIVE-LEVEL DECISIONS THEN... THEN...," he stammered, and, with renewed zeal, shouted, "THEN YOU'RE JUST A WIMP!"

The old man looked at him evenly. "Lower. Not so personal."

Cromwell's voice dropped an octave. "YOUR WORK IS SUB-PAR. I THINK YOU'RE A POOR EXCUSE FOR A MANAGER."

"That voice is better, but the message is wrong," instructed the Maniac. "Try this: YOUR WORK IS SUB-PAR. Pause. We expect more from someone of your caliber."

"YOUR WORK IS SUB-PAR. WE—"

"No—*pause*. You have to pause. Also make the first part stronger: YOUR PERFORMANCE IS POOR. Pause. See? Now you."

"YOU SUCK. We—"

"No, no, no. You can't say 'you suck' to an employee. Try again."

"YOUR WORK IS LOUSY. Pause?"

"Pause, right, go on."

"You suck. Oh, that's not right, I'm sorry, I—"

"Never mind, Cromwell. We'll work on it later."

As Cromwell left, Ernest's eyes were even wider than before, but not from fear. He had suddenly grasped the truth: This was a Minute Gripe as taught by the Master himself. He longed to show his mentor that he understood.

"So that was a lesson in how to deliver the Minute Gripe!" he said.

"You catch on fast, son. I like that. Cromwell should be as bright."

"It simply amazes me that you take the time to guide the underlings with such care. You seem to be so unselfish, so giving of yourself."

"Not really. I tried to get rid of him."

"But when he insisted, you didn't turn him away. How much time do you spend guiding your employees—aside from the weekly meeting?"

"As little as possible. I try to miss the meetings, too."

"You do? Why is that?"

"What an idiotic question! Because I'm interested in saving time, not using it!"

"I'm sorry?"

"It's very simple. I spend all my time saving time."

"You mean you never use your time?"

"Let me illustrate my point." He thrust his large hand deep into his pocket and took out a quarter. This he gave to Ernest. "Now," he continued, "you have a quarter. If you go down to the store and buy a package of gum, you've used that quarter. You no longer have it. It's gone. But if you don't use that quarter, then you've saved it. You can't use it *and* save it! It's the same way with time. Here—this card says it all."

The One Minute Maniac handed the young man a card bearing another pearl of his wisdom:

*

*Use Time
And You
Lose Time*

*To Make Time
You Have To
Fake Time*

*

"It's taken me years to perfect this technique. At first I could only save a scrap or two of time a day. I'd set aside five minutes that I wouldn't use."

"What would you do?"

"Bend paper clips into animals or something."

"Oh. That certainly couldn't be called using your time."

"Exactly. Eventually I worked up to half a day's worth of time that went completely unused. Now, as you can see, I have only a few hours a week— that damned meeting with my employees—when I must use, and therefore waste, my time."

"Amazing. It all seems so simple."

The Great Man leaned back in his chair, gazing at the young man's face. He recognized the expression: half awe, half bewilderment. It was just the effect he had sought to create, one he had seen time and again on the faces of the faithful, and one that he knew must be maintained. When the expression slipped, when the brow furrowed with a question or the head tilted in a thoughtful pose, there lay the danger—the moment when the curtain might be swept aside.

The young man's head, even now, was tilting quizzically. "But...," he began.

"Yes...?" intoned the Great One. His eyebrows arched, ready for the challenge.

"Well, suppose I was a manager. And suppose that although I am enlightened, my employees and my supervisor are not. I deliver a Minute Gripe to my inept assistant. He goes straight to my boss, who calls me on the carpet and makes me apologize to the assistant. My boss then gives the assistant many of what had been my responsibilities. Although the assistant is still technically my subordinate, in reality he spies on me and reports to my boss."

"In response, Ernest, let me ask you a question. How long does it take to brush your teeth?"

"I beg your pardon, sir?"

"Do you think you could save time brushing your teeth?"

"Why, I suppose so."

"There's your answer."

Ernest was confused. "Really, sir, I don't mean to be disrespectful, but I don't see—"

"WHY, IT'S OBVIOUS!" shouted the Maniac. "If you were to cut a little time off brushing your teeth in the morning, you would arrive at work that much sooner. If you could dress a little faster, drive a little faster, do everything a little faster, why, you might arrive at work an hour earlier! You could spend that hour solving your problem."

"But how would I solve it?"

"I have no idea. That's your problem. But you must admit that before you can solve any problem, you must have time to think of a solution. Am I right?"

"Yes, sir."

"There you have it. There is no problem in this world that cannot be solved, given enough time. So getting more time is the first problem to solve. And you'll find out more about that in my new book, *TOTAL MANIA.*"

"But I've read all your books, and I've never heard of that one."

"That's because it's not published yet. But when it is, you'll buy it."

"Yes, I will, sir!" said the young man, and both of them enjoyed a moment of laughter.

But the One Minute Maniac laughed a little longer.

Later, as Ernest was about to leave, the Old Man put a hand on his shoulder, and smiled. "I like your dedication, young fellow. You look like a winner — I'm gonna keep my eye on you."

The two shook hands.

"In fact," continued the Maniac, "I think I'll let you be the first to read the Maniascript of my new book." He handed his grateful visitor a thin manilla envelope. "It took all of last week's ShaveTime to finish and even spilled over into MealTime. It's hard to dictate when you're chewing."

"A whole book?" Ernest exclaimed. "In less than a week? Incredible!"

The Maniac shrugged. "Minutes," he said, "are money."

Ernest rushed home with his precious cargo. What a rare opportunity—the chance to be the first to read the latest teachings of the Master of Minute Mania!

Upon arriving, he announced to his wife "Norma, I can't be disturbed," and locked himself in the study.

He turned eagerly to the first page. . . .

TOTAL MANIA

~

The Great American Lifestyle Makeover

~

by The One Minute Maniac

PREFACE

In my many bestsellers I have told childlike stories illustrating a management style that's simple and time-efficient. These books have sold millions, confirming both the value of Minute Hypes, Gripes, and Scams, and the deep American desire for easy solutions. In this book I move beyond the workplace to present *TOTAL MANIA — The Great American Lifestyle Makeover.*

In my brief introduction, "The Shameful Time Deficit," I describe the wasteful behavior that has driven America to the brink of a time crisis — and how you can benefit from it.

Part One, "Acting Like A Maniac: Timetips," is jam-packed with practical pointers that will make you throb with efficiency, at work and at play.

In Part Two, "Thinking Like A Maniac: Timercises," you'll learn to enjoy FantasyTime while TurboTuning your aura.

And Part Three, "Revolting Like A Maniac: A Call To Frenzy," outlines my five-year plan for reorganizing civilization as we know it. Chapters include the informative, "Your Relaxed Friends— The People's Enemy," and the eye-opening, "How the Time-Wasting Conspiracy Has Duped Our Leaders." If you have young children, don't miss "My Kid's a YAM!"—a complete introduction to the Young American Maniac program.

TOTAL MANIA will change your life so much you won't even recognize it—and America will thank you for it!

A final thought before you begin: Remember, time is like toothpaste—once it's out of the tube, it's a slimy mess and you'll never get it back in again. Join me in squeezing the best out of life. Let's get Manic!

Yours,

The Maniac

INTRODUCTION:
The Shameful Time Deficit

Everyone has heard of America's national debt, described as "massive," "exploding," and "alarming" —like a giant trick cigar. But there is an even more dangerous liability: the soaring National Time Deficit.

Each year Americans waste trillions of hours of time. Did I say trillions? I meant *zillions.* Studies indicate office workers waste more than 60 percent of each workday on unproductive unwork. Many wind up owing their companies time! The scandalous result is sagging American productivity— and a flood of cheap time imported from overseas to meet our huge demand.

In the good old days, Americans consumed American time the American way, with all-American diversions like sandlot baseball, Silly Putty, TV Westerns, surf music, and Mom's apple pie. We worked hard, and made time pay.

Today, Americans not only waste more time than ever before, we also spend a lot more of it on foreign diversions. German cars, Japanese VCRs, French food, Italian design, Brazilian sambas...the list goes on and on. We spend countless hours in musty foreign museums, lying naked on exotic beaches, and cruising aimlessly off alien shores.

Office workers waste more than 60 percent of each workday on unproductive unwork.

The United States now owes foreign nations so much time that even if it worked lunches and weekends it would take forever to pay it all back. And if the time-rich nations of OTEC (the Organization of Time-Exporting Countries) decide to get tough, you can say goodbye to the phony three-hour dentist appointment! People who kill time may *do* time—behind bars.

How can a nation excuse itself when it runs short of time? Can it say it had car trouble, as you or I would? No, it can only point to its people and say, "They did it!"

"That's really terrible, Maniac," some of you are saying, "but what's the bottom line? What's in it for me?" A perfectly natural question for any true American. Sure, *TOTAL MANIA* can boost American productivity and correct the National Time Deficit. But the real payoff—let's face it—is getting you on the fast track to the mega-buck good life!

Acting Like A Maniac: TIMETIPS

This section tells you all you need to know to accelerate your life, without getting bogged down in time-wasting theory. Everything is listed alphabetically—just pick a topic and go.

I suggest cutting photocopies of these pages into neat pieces, each one containing a Timetip. Tape a couple to your shoes each morning for reference, and you'll always start off on the right foot!

ANGER

It's often said that to control your temper you should count to 10 when angry. But using the standard decimal system is a waste of time. Use a binary system, and get calm faster — just count 0, 1, 10.

BACKLOG

When you have a backlog of items on your "To Do" list, eliminate them using this simple trick:

Think of some information you need to complete the item — the harder to get, the better. Invent this requirement if you have to. Then think of someone you can make responsible for it.

Give that person a call, and explain that you must have their input before you can continue. Calling more than one person for a critical contribution is even better. They'll be irritated, but impressed by your thoroughness. Don't forget to end by saying, "The ball's in your court." And be sure to let your superiors know what's delaying the task.

After this, one of three things will happen. (1) The others will decide it's easier for them to do the whole thing themselves. (2) It will take so long to get the information the item will no longer be worth doing. (3) They'll call back with the information — whereupon you simply ask for more.

With this method and a few phone calls, you can eliminate dozens of those minute-robbing items on your "To Do" list.

BOREDOM

Everyone is bored at one time or another, but few people optimize boredom by planning for it. Instead, they waste time by being bored and accomplishing nothing else. Plan your boredom so that it doesn't interrupt important activities. Like investment analysis, or sex.

Instead, schedule boredom for periods when you will be fulfilling unpleasant obligations: a visit to a sick friend or a meeting with a client, for example. Or sex.

BATHROOM HABITS

Going to the bathroom can really cut into your day. Don't let it—use that time!

For men: Attaching double-sided adhesive tape to the back of your Minute Planner will allow you to mount it above a urinal you're using. With your free hand, you can jot down ideas and notes that you might otherwise forget.

Women, of course, may simply place their planners on their laps.

CHILDREN

Children can consume vast amounts of your time unless you plan wisely. Here are a few tips:

When you plan your family, arrange to have your children born as close together as possible. They'll go through diapers, school, puberty, and drug problems at roughly the same time, and you won't have to waste time readjusting your technique for each crisis.

When a baby cries, wait until you're sure that it's wet, hungry, and tired all at the same time. You can then change it, feed it, and put it down for a nap with a minimum of time expended.

Pillowcases with a hole cut in the top make quick and colorful infant wear. They can be used until a child can dress itself.

Never make lunches for school children! This wastes your time and spoils the child. Give your son or daughter a dollar and encourage them to strike a deal with kids who do bring lunches. A great way to save time while teaching them there's no such thing as a free lunch.

When having dinner, insist that your children talk with their mouths full. You can catch up on their news without having to wait for all that chewing.

After dinner, you can wash the smaller children at the same time you wash the dishes, if you're using a double sink. Might as well wash the family dog while you're at it.

When it comes time to explain
the facts of life, replace the traditional
lengthy heart-to-heart talk
with a few tasteful adult magazines.

If you often work late (and what Maniac doesn't?), you might not have time to see your children as much as you'd like. To remedy this, have your spouse videotape the little rug rats so you can keep up with their hijinks. It's a heart-warming way to cap the 11 o'clock news, plus you can fast-forward past the dull parts. Have your secretary at work tape your activities as well, so the urchins can see how successful their mom and dad are becoming.

When it comes time to explain the facts of life, replace the traditional lengthy heart-to-heart talk with a few tasteful adult magazines.

CLOTHING

Most people take too much time dressing. A good solution is to sew an entire outfit together.

MEN: Sew your boxer shorts into gray slacks and then stitch a white shirt to the waistband. Leave a tie permanently tied under the collar, and you have an outfit you can wiggle into in under three minutes.

WOMEN: Substitute panty hose, gray skirt and white blouse in the above outfit.

Not only will this scheme speed up DressTime but it also saves closet space and simplifies your laundry—no more tedious clothes-sorting.

Advanced Maniacs will want to dress in layers for the day's different activities: overcoat and galoshes over office wear over aerobic wear over evening wear over sleepwear.

COMPETITION

Unfortunately, there are always a few employees who let ambition affect their performance of your duties. Minute Gripes, Hypes, and Scams are essential, but they may not be enough. Try distracting them with performance anxiety: encourage rivalry, for example, by assigning the same task to several of them at once. Keep deadlines rigid, and difficult or impossible to meet. Mention survival of the fittest and other laws of the jungle. Use phrases like "There's no room for dinosaurs in this office" and "a bonus to the first person to steal all of Fink's accounts!"

CONVERSATION CUT-OFFS

How often does someone waste your time with a long, drawn-out discourse, droning on and on, ignoring your signals to get to the point or put a cork in it? Probably far too often, simply because you're afraid of "offending" them.

This is just what the problem talker counts on. People who like to hear themselves talk are compensating for how intensely boring they are. They may know this, and they may know you know this, but they would rather believe no one knows it, and are betting you won't tell them.

Here are two approaches the One Minute Maniac uses to stop gab in its tracks:

The Subtle Approach Remember, you don't have to deflate a windbag to keep him from blowing. Give him a plausible reason for shutting up, and you'll both be happy. Try one of these:

"Don't let me take up any more of your time. I know someone in your critical position is extremely busy, so I'll let you get back to work." (This works for everyone down to the guy who sweeps the mailroom.)

(Coughing heavily) "You'd better leave — I'm having an attack. Doctor says it's a miracle I'm not dead."

"While you're here, maybe you'd like to see my vacation slides. I'm documenting manhole covers in cities around the world. It'll just take a minute to set things up."

"By the way, my kid's school is selling chocolate-covered hardboiled eggs to raise money. Can I put you down for a couple of cartons?"

"So you're in sales? What a coincidence, so am I! Step right in — my Tupperware party starts in five minutes!"

"Say, wasn't that your car that was stolen from the garage this morning?"

The Direct Approach If you can afford to offend, try these surefire methods:

Simply stop talking and stare silently at the other person until he or she leaves the room, completely unnerved.

Look the blabbermouth in the eye and tell her life is too short to keep talking to her.

Stuff his tie in his mouth.

CONVERSATION CUT-OFFS

DELEGATING

The secret to successful delegating is to teach subordinates to do your job while intimidating them from any thought of rising to your level. Don't mistake this for selfishness. After all, you're giving them the satisfaction of achieving on their own, with laughably little help from you. They will learn how to make it up as they go along—just as you do. This kind of opportunity is invaluable. Really, they should be paying you for the privilege!

DRIVING

To be an efficient time manager, you must own a car with an automatic transmission. This ensures a free foot and a free hand at all times. With a little practice, you can use your foot to load motivational lecture tapes into your cassette deck. With your free hand you can jot down ideas and notes you might otherwise forget.

A creative approach to steering will free your hands for more important things.

GOALS

It is essential that goals be well defined. Most people's goals are not. For example, many people entertain a vague goal such as "Someday I'd like to get married and have a family."

With a little thought, you can see that these are actually two goals that normally require two different approaches.

But if you want to achieve both goals efficiently, you can combine them by marrying someone recently widowed or divorced who already has children. Obituaries and local gossip offer quick leads here.

If, on the other hand, you only want to get married, the state of Nevada offers the most sensible wedding requirements, time-managementwise.

MEETINGS, ATTENDING

Meetings are unavoidable, and most have less spark than a narcolepsy clinic. A dynamic One Minute Maniac can make a big difference. (This difference will be largely an illusion, since you'll use the time to consider more challenging matters — like how your coworkers would look bowling naked.)

The skilled Maniac will appear completely involved in the meeting, and comment occasionally to maintain the illusion. Brief, punchy comments suggest acute wisdom:

"That's the upside."
"What's the downside?"
"We need to get up to speed."
"How about downtime?"
"I won't put up with that."
"Let's take it downtown."
"That's not up to you."
"Sez who?"
"Sez me."
"Wanna step outside?"
"Make me."
"I don't make trash, I burn it."

And so on....

If discussion strays from the matter at hand, a strong, clear signal from you will get it back on track and earn you the respect of your coworkers. A starter's pistol works very well, although some Maniacs prefer to use a duck call or whoopee cushion.

If a meeting seems unfocused, demand to know what it's supposed to accomplish. In the absence of a clear purpose or strong leadership, consider leading a mutiny or coup d'etat. If it's a minor meeting, install a teenage intern as leader, freeing you to leave entirely.

MEETINGS, ESCAPING

Decide how much time you're willing to give to your next meeting, then set your wristwatch alarm accordingly. (If you don't have an alarm watch, use an egg timer with a loud dinger.) When it goes off, everyone will assume you have a pressing obligation. Affecting an air of deep responsibility and devotion to duty, rise and head out the door. (As in prison escapes, don't run unless they start shooting.)

This gambit shouldn't require more than a mumbled "excuse me," but if you care to elaborate when the alarm goes off, here are a few successful examples:

"I have to catch my broker before the Tokyo Exchange closes."

"My staff is brainstorming upstairs. I'm the lightning rod."

"Gotta get the football pool odds into the overnight pouch."

"I hate to be pedestrian, but I have to feed my parking meter."

"I've got a six-way conference call coming in on a satellite uplink. Scotty says he can't hold on much longer."

MULTITASKING

Like sophisticated software, a One Minute Maniac must be able to perform several tasks at once. Why be content to just talk on the phone when at the same time you can be dictating a memo, speedreading your mail, listening to an underling's report, signing letters, and enjoying an office manicure?

NATURAL DISASTER

If a natural or unnatural disaster (e.g., a hurricane or a nerve gas leak) threatens your hometown, don't leave until the very last minute. Because your business associates will be busy running for their lives, you can get the jump on them. Leave messages on their answering machines asking them to attend tomorrow's important meeting with armloads of reports.

When they get back in town, they will be impressed with your dedication in the face of disaster and, out of guilt, will allow you any amount of time you need to revise your report for the meeting. This is actually a variation of creating PanicTime (see entry).

TURBO-NETWORKING

NETWORKING

Everyone knows the value of Networking, or getting down to business in social situations after a few pleasantries have been exchanged. But most people are too roundabout in their approach, even in this fairly direct example: "Mr. Skivey, I'd like you to meet Ms. Tosterwheel, Executive Vice President in charge of Residual Sludge Conversion at Hoop, Hoop and Dinker. She's a graduate of Toxic Tech, and a gifted croquet player."

"Very nice to meet you, Ms. Tosterwheel. I shoot a mean wicket myself. By the way, I'm in sludge as well. My firm manufactures Roto-Sludge Supreme. Have you seen our new line?"

This sort of jaw-wagging belongs to a bygone age. A more efficient response would be: "Glad to know you—how can you help me?"

ONE MINUTE PHONING

Some people spend more time talking on the phone than sleeping. If they could have it surgically implanted, they would. Not a bad idea, but unnecessary with today's cordless and cellular telephones. The One Minute Maniac himself always has a multiline phone within reach, but he never lets other people waste his time on it.

Fortunately, many of the aforementioned techniques and evasions (see *Conversation Cutoffs*) can also be used to trim phone talk. But don't neglect the unique power a phone gives you. Since your caller can't see what's happening at your end, you can invent freely. These examples should inspire you:

"Oh my God! Madge, I gotta go. Our canary just burst into flames!"

"Whoa—what's going on here? Feels like an earthquake! Later, babe."

"I'd love to hear more about your kid's festering boils, but I've got two calls on hold and someone in my office waiting."

"Annuity insurance? Fascinating! Send me a brochure and I'll get back to you."

"Sorry, I have to keep this line free for an important call. My husband's watching Dialing for Dollars."

An alarm from your watch or some other device can help shut off the monotonous flood of words from your caller if you follow it with a snappy excuse:

"Oh, no—must be another bomb threat. Gotta run."

"That's my pager—they need me to come in and sew up that new account." (This one not recommended for doctors.)

"Sounds like an intruder's gotten through our security perimeter. It's Rambo Time—cover me, I'm going in!"

Or crinkle cellophane into the receiver while saying, "What a rotten connection—we'd better wrap this up."

Keep a piece of fabric handy to cover the mouthpiece so you can disguise your voice to avoid time-wasters like salespeople and your mother.

ONE-MINUTE PHONING

Don't settle for just a day at a glance.
Schedule every minute
and leave nothing to chance.

With Minute Planning
your day will run like clockwork.

ONE MINUTE PLANNING

For the One Minute Maniac, standard daily planners are as useful as sundials. Instead, have your own 24-sheet-per-day planner specially printed, with a page for each hour, broken down into minutes and seconds.

PANICTIME

When you need more time than you have to prepare for a meeting, the solution is to create PanicTime for whomever you are meeting with. Call them up and say, "Of course, I assume you will be bringing with you a full report on the cost-efficiency factorization of the environmental impact measures as they relate to the five-year corporate goalplan."

Not wanting to appear unprepared, your victim will probably respond, "Of course." After he thinks about it, however, he will probably call you back and beg to meet at a later date. You will reluctantly agree. Remind yourself of this technique by jotting down "create PanicTime for Mr. Jones" in your Minute Planner.

REPETITIVE LEARNING
Remember the Value of Repetitive Learning.
Remember the Value of ·Repetitive Learning.
Remember the Value of Repetitive Learning.
Remember the Value of Repetitive Learning.
Remember the Value of Repetitive Learning.
Remember the Value of Repetitive Learning.
Remember the Value of Repetitive Learning.
Remember the Value of Repetitive Learning.
Remember the Value of Repetitive Learning.
Remember the Value of Repetitive Learning.

(Repeat as necessary)

RESPONSES (to Minute Gripes)
The greatest waste of time when giving an employee a Minute Gripe is listening to their excuses. Don't do it! Remember that every moment you spend listening to someone else is a moment lost forever. A Minute Gripe can become a Micro Gripe. Here's an example:

"Frank, you screwed up the Smedley account."
"I know, sir, I—"
"Get it?"
"Of course, what I—"
"Got it?"
"Yes, that is—"
"Good—personwise, you're okay, Frank."
"Thank you, sir. I—"
"Back to work now."
"Y-y-yes sir."

TOTAL ELAPSED TIME: 14.8 SECONDS

RETRO PLANS

Why waste time planning for an uncertain future? Create your strategic plans after the fact, anticipating brilliantly whatever happened. You will be acclaimed for your on-target projections, your accurate estimates of the capital, manpower, and materials required, and your foresight in having prepared a contingency plan for those unexpected developments. And, of course, a Retro Plan requires just a fraction of the time needed to prepare a plan for things that haven't yet occurred!

RUMORS

Take time to learn about your more difficult coworkers. Ask Personnel to check into potentially dangerous background rumors that cast doubt on their competence and morality. If you haven't heard any, make them up. Remember, today's rumor may be tomorrow's fact!

SEX

In the fifties, everyone talked about repressed sex. In the sixties, everyone talked about free sex. In the seventies, everyone talked about good sex. Now it's the eighties—let's talk about *fast* sex.

Like it or not, sex takes too much time. To be a true maniac, all those elaborate positions must go. The same for unscheduled lovemaking, chance encounters, and strangers in the night. Less *can* be more. Keep it short and sweet.

SHAVING

ShaveTime can and should be made more productive. For example: When you are shaving, use your free hand to brush your teeth. This goes for women, too. A great timesaver.

SHOUTING

Don't let a few yards' distance keep you from conversing. Just raise your voice several decibels. For example, when meeting a business acquaintance at an airport you can start negotiations by shouting at him as he walks off the plane.

Shouting also brings quicker attention from service personnel, such as secretaries, waiters and attorneys. It's also a great way to improve communications with your family around the house.

Check your Minute Planner, and see if you can't save time by blocking out a few minutes here and there as ShoutTime.

SLEEP

SleepTime is a tremendous waste, but no one can safely advise you to avoid sleep completely.

The best way to schedule SleepTime is to compress it. That is, work without sleep until you are exhausted, and then rest until your energy is restored. Some One Minute Maniacs I know go for 20 days or more without sleep and then book a few days in their community hospital to recover. This simple technique makes them more productive than many Third World nations.

SHOUTTIME

SPEEDCHATTING

The Low-Fat Chat More than a third of the average conversation is fat. Inside every fat conversation is a lean one crying to get out. Remember, the fewer the words, the greater the authority. The following comparison shows how even a seemingly focused exchange can be streamlined:

"May I please speak to Mr. Franklin Prescott in Corporate Finance?"	"Gimme Frank Prescott."
"Please hold just a minute, sir, and I'll connect you to him."	"Hang on."
"This is Franklin Prescott, vice president of corporate finance."	"Frank Prescott."
"Mr. Prescott, my name is Joseph Bamboozle. I am vice president of client relations at Society Debentures, Incorporated."	"Hi, Frank. Joe Bamboozle of Society Debs.
"I'm afraid I'm not familiar with your company, Mr. Bamboozle. What may I do for you?"	"So?"

"We. are a top-rated firm specializing in first-time public stock offerings and private-placement financing."

"Wanna float some corporate paper?

"Unfortunately, we've recently concluded a leveraged buyout with complete recapitilization, including a package of long-term convertible debentures. We have no need for additional capital at present."

"Naw, we're flush."

"I quite understand, Mr. Prescott. If you don't object, I'd like to take the liberty of sending you some information on my company and its services for future reference.

"Too bad. I'll send ya some info anyway."

"Please do. I'd like to learn more about Society Debentures, and I'll keep the material on file. We hope that future success will increase our capital requirements and necessitate further expansion."

"Why not—you never know."

"Well, congratulations on your successful buyout, and best wishes for a prosperous future."

"Right. Knock 'em dead."

"Thank you, Mr. Bamboozle."

"You bet."

"And thanks for discussing your situation with me, Mr. Prescott."

"Nice talking."

"You're very welcome. I'll let you know if anything develops."

"Sure. Later."

"I'd appreciate it.   "Bye."
Goodbye."

The conversation on the right is direct and efficient, lean but not mean, and takes much less time than the overstuffed dialogue on the left. And I don't have to tell you which one is more American.

You should eliminate irrelevant chitchat, needless courtesy, idle pleasantries, and pretentious jargon from all your conversations. Not only will you save bundles of time, but others will respect and envy your savvy, efficient style of communication.

You will find that speedchatting benefits personal expression even more. Here's an example, along with its lean counterpart:

"Hello, darling. You
know, when I woke up
this morning and
realized that I had to
get out of our warm
bed and go to work, I
realized how much I'd
rather stay with you.
I'd rather have your
arms around me than
be fighting rush-hour
traffic, just to punch
the clock. Last night

seemed extra special.
Maybe I was just in a
romantic mood—after
that great dinner
you made, and the
wine...I don't know,
but I do know you're
becoming a big part of
my life. It's not like I
was even looking for
someone to fall in love
with! We've both been
through this before,
and I don't want to
rush things, but since
we've been spending
'most every weekend
together anyway, what
would you say to
moving in with me?
Please think about it,
anyway. It's something
I've been thinking
about. Well, that's
what l called for—just
to say I missed you.
And to see if I could
entice you into moving
in! Let me know how
you feel. I love you,
darling. Bye."

"Babe! Last night
was a 10! Wanna
shack up?"

SPEEDREADING

With the stock of knowledge in the world doubling every two years, it's impossible to stay abreast of new developments—so don't try. Read only reviews and summaries of material (better still, reviews of reviews and summaries of summaries), memorizing the latest buzzwords and catchphrases. The new ideas themselves can be ignored.

Of course, a true Maniac speedreads everything and requires his employees to do the same. When speedreading, however, remember not to move your lips—sprained lips are painful, and not a pretty sight.

TAPE RECORDERS

Use a tape recorder to master special information through repetition. This allows you to absorb important material by playing it back at opportune times—for example, when driving your car, shopping, or attending a funeral. This method is perfect for motivational tapes, of course, but overdoing it may lead to hypermotivation, resulting in truly vicious corporate politics. (There's nothing wrong with that, but the resulting bloodshed has given hypermotivation a bad name.) Used with care, repeated exposure to the right stuff can make you a well-programmed whiz kid.

Thinking Like A Maniac: *TIMERCISES*

Many people allow Time to rule them, when they should be masters of Time. These simple meditations will help you increase your Timastery. Choose one Timercise a day. Lie quietly, and repeat the mantra of One Minute Mania: O-M-M, O-M-M, OMM, OMM. Then ponder these thoughts:

PREHISTORIC TIMERCISE

Imagine you are living in the caveman era, when Time was totally obscure. Because Time was so poorly defined, vast amounts of it were wasted (a horrifying thought). Time was moody and unreliable. It often quarreled with its close companion, Space. Their arguments were marked by cataclysmic events: ice ages, reversal of the earth's poles, collisions of astral bodies. When they became very angry, Space would collapse and Time would run backward.

Just imagine what that could do to a well-planned schedule! Not to mention trying to save time when no one even grasped the concept. Nobody cared when you got stuck in the primordial ooze, or had to wait forever (Ha–"forever"!) at a dinosaur crossing.

Think about that, and be glad you live in an age when everyone keeps an eye on Time, and it behaves itself.

MIND OVER TIMERCISE

Do you fear time? Are you always running late, juggling appointments, postponing what you should be doing (or worse, what you really want to do)?

Don't let Time push you around! You can regain a sense of Timastery through symbolic action. Buy a few cheap digital timepieces and find new meaning in the phrase "to kill time."

A simple hammer can provide fast relief. Use it to smash a clock in the face. See? That wasn't so hard, and it felt great, didn't it?

Tired of seeing time fly? How about watching it fry—sautéing in butter and garlic over a high flame, turning golden brown, then black, then stinking a lot. You don't care. The next time you order a burger with the works, specify digital or analog.

Choose any method that seems appropriate. Does yardwork take too much of your time? Mulch a timepiece with your mower. Are you spending the best years of your life caught in rush-hour traffic? Keep several cheap watches in your glove compartment and crunch them under your wheels in the old stop-and-go. Is household management an endless drag? Try running a clock through a blender, a toaster, a dishwasher, or all three. Is your computer gobbling up your precious moments? Torture it by resetting its clock to April, 1904—a time before it was invented.

These actions will help liberate you from your fear of time. Break through those old attitudes and make time work for you.

HYPER TIMERCISE

Don't let fear of authority stand between you and Timastery. Imaginative Timercises like this one can cut authority figures down to size.

Einstein's theory of relativity tells us that time becomes slower as we approach the speed of light. Imagine being able to work at hyperspeed, leaving all those nagging irritations and delaying obstacles behind. Think of it—you can do more in one minute than your boss can do in hours at his usual, plodding earth pace.

Now imagine your boss talking to you. Speaking with infinite slowness, he asks you to have a report on the Higgins account ready tomorrow morning. Before he can finish his sentence, you, with your endless supply of time, research his entire past. You visit his hometown, learn every detail of his life, and return with enough incriminating evidence to destroy his career forever. As the last word leaves his lips, you announce that you will complete the report when you see fit, or you will reveal to the world his sordid past.

EROTIC TIMERCISE

Oooh, baby. If you have to ask, you may not be Maniac material. Let's face it—dazzling financial and career success is not enough motivation for everyone. (They should be, but it's an imperfect world.) Those men and women who insist on seeing Timastery as a means to some romantic end should try this Timercise.

First, visualize mouth-watering members of whichever sex you find appealing. (I realize some of you have trouble visualizing anything else.) They are vivid in your mind's eye—sexy, charming, bright, witty. They would probably never even notice you under normal conditions. But you have mastered the methods of One Minute Mania. You move with a supple grace, you speak and act with no excess effort, you manipulate others with laughable ease.

Imagine how admiring and, yes, affectionate, the objects of your desire become as they bask in the aura of your Timastery. You are irresistible. And thanks to One Minute Mania, you have plenty of time to enjoy this fantasy. Go ahead. I'll hold your calls.

SANDS OF TIMERCISE

Visualize an enormous, old-fashioned hourglass. Imagine the top of it filled with all the sand in the Sahara, times ten. This is your personal hourglass, and the sand represents Time itself. Now imagine yourself as the Ruler of Time, able to control the flow of sand into the bottom of the hourglass, from a trickle to a torrent. Look—there, in the bottom chamber, is a huge horde of people. Recognize them? Those are the people who cause delays in your life and waste your time (it often seems to be their sole purpose). They're all in the hourglass: long-winded colleagues, sullen waiters, rubbernecking drivers, demanding relatives, and countless more—you know who they are.

Go ahead—open the gate and dump on them for a change. Watch as this inconsiderate crowd coughs in your hourglass sandstorm. Perhaps burying them in the sands of Time will teach them to respect every fleeting minute. Look at them now, gasping and crying for mercy, swearing they've learned their lesson. Don't bet on it—but stop the sand anyway. They've wasted enough of your time.

NO BIG DEAL TIMERCISE

Imagine that you are totally unimportant. Utterly insignificant. So unworthy of attention that you are, for all purposes, invisible. No one gives a flying farthing what you do. Because of this, you now have all the time you want to do anything you want. A useful meditation when pressure is high.

BIG DEAL TIMERCISE

Imagine you are incredibly important. You are the most important entity in the universe, so awesome that you are unapproachable. The masses must guess your desires, and make offerings to you—from afar, of course, for it is unthinkable that you should waste your time dealing with them. You ignore others. You now have all the time you want to do anything you want. Also useful when pressure is high.

LIFEATHON TIMERCISE

The One Minute Maniac knows that life is a race. Every man has his own lifeathon to run. But don't believe you're only competing with yourself. You're running against a vast number of people who seem intent on getting in your way and slowing you down.

Imagine running your entire lifeathon held back by this dull-witted herd. How can you win? Try running smarter: Get behind people who will cut through resistance and work to your advantage. Run around the others, who are destined to fall by the wayside.

You're breathing more easily now. At last you're in the fast lane, where you've always belonged. Others are scrambling to get out of your way. Many are cheering you on! You have the aura of a winner. Nothing can stop you now—you're a One Minute Maniac!

UTOPIAN TIMERCISE

This is the most difficult Timercise of them all: *Imagine you are relaxed.* You are sitting on your couch at home with your shoes off and your feet up on the coffee table. Your kids are in bed. Your spouse is on a business trip. The TV is off. You don't have anything to do. You stretch, you're getting ready to enjoy this time to yourself. You're almost ready to enjoy it. You'll start enjoying it in just a minute. You count down the seconds until the enjoyment begins...10...9...8...7...6 ...wait, you have to scratch your elbow. You start over...10...9...8...the phone rings...10... 9...the tap is dripping—oh, forget it! On second thought, this Timercise is impossible.

HANDS OF TIMERCISE

You are hanging from the hands of a large clock at the top of a very high building. As you struggle to keep from falling to your death, King Kong appears....

E*RNEST read on, deep into the night....*

few manic months later....

Ernest Hits The
Deck Running

Ernest awoke instantly to the brisk strains of a military march on his cassette alarm. His wife Norma groaned and turned over, clamping the pillow over her head. Her initial respect for his time-efficiency drive had recently given way to irritation, and it saddened him to think that Norma just might not be able to keep up.

He punched on a tape of pulsating ExecuCise music and began bobbing vigorously up and down before the mirror as he shaved. This was the Office Squat ExecuCise for dynamic sitting—so vital to good chairmanship. With his free hand he did Telephone Curls, pausing occasionally to jot down a note to himself on the waterproof pad he carried even in the shower. Before he met the Maniac, Ernest used to ease into the day as if entering a hot bath, too distracted to focus his thoughts, much less make note of them. Just thinking of the wasted time and lost inspiration made him shudder.

He had taken the Maniac's teachings to heart, and come up with some Timetips of his own. The multiple high-pressure shower heads he'd installed had greatly reduced RinseTime (although Norma complained it was like standing buck naked in a monsoon). Industrial hot-air blowers allowed him to dry himself and style his hair in seconds, even while splashing on a bit of after-shave, applying skin lotion, and trimming his nails.

Ernest pulled on one of his all-together outfits— socks, underwear, and shirt with knotted tie all sewed into a three-piece gray flannel suit. He felt as keen as a fireman leaping into his uniform for a night alarm. Which reminded him: Norma was resisting his plan to add a firepole to the stairwell, just as she'd resisted his other time-saving changes.

But she had to admit their house was now a cutting-edge example of ultra-low-maintenance design—a blend of high-impact laminates, heavy-traffic upholstery, energy-efficient halogen lighting, and other hyphenated synthetics. Entire rooms could be cleaned rapidly with any recognized spray cleaner, or simply hosed down. True, they'd lost the cat during the first hose-down, and little Tommy still asked them, "Where's Fluffy?" But that was the price of progress, wasn't it?

The neighbors had been slow to understand his crusade. Some of them were still angry about the time Ernest had gone astray on his riding mower, driving across a large flower bed, a newly seeded lawn, and a prize cactus garden.

He admitted that the motivational tapes had been too loud in his headphones, and the tanning reflector had narrowed his vision, but, hey, it could have happened to anyone! It was a good thing in the end, because it had inspired him to replace the grass with easy-care artificial turf. And still some people complained, no doubt resenting the new lawn's eternal perfection. He was surrounded by petty humans and stupid machines (and vice versa – the smart machines could be petty, too).

THE COMPLEAT COMMUTER

Ernest left the house at 5:22 A.M. sharp. At this hour, with no interference from other drivers, he was able to hold to a speed carefully calculated to avoid red lights. Norma was sleeping in again. "My little slugabed," he thought affectionately, but with a trace of concern at his wife's lack of discipline. She just didn't understand the thrill of beating rush-hour traffic. At first Norma had tried to follow her husband's example, but her resolve soon weakened, and she began questioning the value of his reforms. Just last night, she had argued with him about starting Tommy in a combination piano/typing class. Ernest was certain it would give the two-year-old a competitive edge, but Norma thought it would be too much too soon.

"You're coddling the boy, Norma," he told her.

"And you want to turn him into a little Maniac!" she shouted. "Screw efficiency!" She continued in this vein for a while, but he refused to waste time arguing. When he went to bed she was drinking brandy and abusing the microwave oven with bits of aluminum foil.

Ernest put these thoughts aside as he settled in to enjoy the drive through the dark, deserted city. His special trip computer kept him company with myriad digital dials, all aglow with continuous readings of miles traveled, miles remaining, miles per hour, miles per gallon, gallons per mile, gallons per hour, hours per gallon, gallons remaining, temperature and humidity both inside and outside the car, and current time in seven world capitals to the hundredth of a second. Into the car's cassette deck Ernest popped one of the Maniac's instructional tapes, recorded to play back at high speed for higher, faster enlightenment. It was very effective, and he didn't mind that it sounded like Alvin and the Chipmunks.

He thought with pride of the incredible success he had achieved using the Maniac's methods. He had risen with astonishing speed through the ranks of CanSys, leaping in a matter of weeks from Junior Entity to Entity Overlord to Director of Streamlining to Vice President of Overt Operations. His story was proof of the Maniac's Inverse Responsibility Law—he now supervised 500 people with less effort than it had once taken him to oversee five

Ernest's efficiency allowed him to do as much work as any other executive in a fraction of the time, and his skillful use of Minute Scams, Minute Hypes, and Minute Gripes had molded his subordinates into a smoothly operating, well-programmed machine.

His fellow employees had complained at first about every one of Ernest's changes—about the enormous, beeping clocks he'd had installed in offices, break areas, and restrooms; about his demand that all written reports be short enough to fit on a large Post-It; about his rule that oral reports be limited to one minute; about his practice of firing a starter's pistol at meetings when discussion strayed. They accused Ernest of taking himself too seriously. He replied, "If I don't take myself too seriously, who will?"

When Ernest issued a company-wide memo about the need to "find the hidden half hour" lost every day through sloppy time management, one wise-cracking manager organized search-and-rescue teams that roamed the office, looking under coffee cups and demanding, "Gotta minute? We're missing several." Ernest did not enjoy being a laughingstock, and he saw to it that that witty guy was now a file clerk in CanSys's Beirut office. How could anyone not see the brilliance of One Minute Mania? It had turbo-charged the entire corporation. And everyone knew Ernest was responsible for the change!

His wristwatch alarm beeped. Time to wind his spiritual mainspring. He popped a cassette entitled "Meditate with the Maniac" into the car's tape player. After the hyperventilation exercise, Ernest practiced visualizing inner TimePeace. As the sun rose above the horizon like a fiery clock face, he chanted the mantra of the One Minute Maniac: "O-M-M...O-M-M...O-M-M..."

STRESS FOR SUCCESS

Ernest rode the express elevator to his spacious office in CanSys World Headquarters. By the time other employees began arriving at work, Ernest had already made numerous calls and processed several stacks of the sort of material that clogs office cogs across the land. In addition to the mandatory Minute Memos, he had subordinates provide summaries of any document longer than a summary.

If it appealed to him he would speed-read the summarized material. If really pressed for time, he would speed-read every third word. In this way Ernest could whip through bushels of correspondence, reports, business magazines, newsletters, and catalogues in less time than an ordinary manager might devote to a middling wine list.

He followed the Maniac's dictum that perceived power increases as desktop items decrease. Ernest's desk fairly radiated power. It was a massive granite-top pedestal whose vast expanse bore only a programmable clock/telephone, a streamlined unit that made the Concorde look boxy. (He always used the speakerphone, with the reverb on high, to keep his hands free and his callers off balance.) Let lesser managers clutter their desks with useless knick-knacks and debris—photos of loved ones, flowers, mutant paperweights, messy "organizers," and on and on. He was made of leaner, meaner stuff.

There wasn't even an in- or out-box, since Ernest disposed almost instantly of any paper to cross his desk. Sometimes he scribbled a brief instruction on the material and put it in a pneumatic tube that sucked it out of his office, firing it into his secretary's in-box. More often he fed it to the heavy-duty paper shredder that lived beside his desk.

Ernest took great pleasure in shredding anything that didn't absolutely need to be filed (including his tie, until he'd gotten the hang of the machine). Certain mean-spirited colleagues had suggested that CanSys could boost its quarterly dividend simply by recycling all the paper that went through Ernest's shredder.

Ironically, some of the most sensitive documents were spared from the shredder's razor teeth and kept locked in his office cabinet. These were the background files on Ernest's coworkers. He believed in taking the time to learn about those he worked with. It helped him understand and correct negative attitudes to One Minute Mania. Now, as he examined the file for Ivan Slack, Ernest was disappointed to find nothing out of the ordinary. Slack was a young outside management consultant hired by CanSys's Executive Committee to observe various company operations. But despite his spotless background, Slack showed a disturbing lack of appreciation for One Minute Mania.

Ernest had spent precious time explaining precious time to the hotshot consultant. He believed he had demonstrated beyond a doubt that time accounting was as important as cost accounting, and that the Maniac's methods were vital to the bottom line. It was all so obvious! Slack took careful notes, but chuckled as he wrote.

The day after Ernest mentioned that he taped notes to himself for later reference, Ivan Slack showed up with numerous bits of paper stuck to his pinstripe suit with adhesive tape. Ernest sputtered, "I meant use a tape recorder!" which only made Slack laugh harder. Was the guy a mental defective, or what?

Slack was annoying, but he would soon be moving on to some other area. It was some comfort knowing that once Timastery courses were required in all business schools, MBAs like Slack would be a thing of the past. Ernest was more concerned with the Retro Plan he was scheduled to complete this morning. Ms. Minion, his executive assistant, had already taken the standard format, plugged in the correct statements and figures for the quarter just ended, and given him the draft.

Working with his accustomed speed, Ernest skimmed the plan, added a few sentences that brilliantly anticipated what had in fact occurred, and altered some of the figures—just to give it a human touch. Now, in a fraction of the time it might have taken to draft a strategic plan with reasonably accurate projections for the future, he had produced a Retro Plan with projections (retrojections, actually) that were far more impressive in their keen foresight and accuracy. So acclaimed were Ernest's strategic plans that no one minded that they never appeared before the fact.

When Ms. Minion entered his office to receive the completed Retro Plan, she couldn't conceal her distress.

"Is something wrong, Ms. Minion?" Ernest asked.

"No, sir—that is, maybe, sir."

"Can you give me a quick rundown?"

"Oh, it's probably nothing, just one of those silly rumors."

"A rumor?"

"Yes, Mr. Fellow. It's going around the company that the Executive Committee is about to launch a new fat-cutting campaign."

"I see," said Ernest, trying not to show his satisfaction that the Committee had finally heeded his proposals to prune some deadwood. "And you're worried about your job?"

"Well...I can't help it, with Joe laid off and all those medical bills for Joe Junior's organ transplant piling up."

"You have nothing to fear, Ms. Minion. Nada. Zippo. Less than zero. My staff is the most efficient in the corporation, the envy of every other executive. And you're a model employee, with excellent taste in clothes." Ernest smiled broadly and gave Ms. Minion's arm a squeeze of reassurance.

"Oh, thank you, Mr. Fellow. I'm sorry I even mentioned it. I'm afraid my anxiety about my family's financial situation is starting to get to me. Have you come to any decision about my raise, sir?" The assistant blinked back tears as she voiced the question.

"I'm afraid giving you a raise during a cost-cutting drive would undermine the credibility of this entire office. It would just play into the hands of our critics. I'm sure you understand, Ms. Minion," Ernest explained, gently but firmly.

"Y-y-yes, sir. I guess I see your point. I'll just pray that they don't repossess Joe Junior's organ."

"Good idea. Here's the Retro Plan—I know you have plenty of work to do, so I'll let you get back to it."

"Yes, Mr. Fellow."

As Ms. Minion left Ernest's office, he regretted that their talk had put him a couple of minutes behind schedule. He was leading a staff meeting set to begin at 10:18. Ernest always specified unusual meeting times to emphasize the need for precision and punctuality. Anyone who was more than a minute late was subjected to a condensed Minute Gripe and required to limit his comments to half the usual 60 seconds. Ernest refused to waste time on latecomers or people who didn't get to the point.

His phone went off like the futuristic air-raid siren it resembled. "Ernest Fellow," he answered. "The meter's running."

It was Norma. "Ernest, we have to talk. The Bo-Peep NeuroTyke Center called. They say Tommy is disrupting the Dynaplay period again. And this morning he threw a tantrum in French finger-painting class. Last week he poured his Protein Punch into a classroom computer. I really think he needs to be in a more relaxed environment."

"Honey, he's just got to learn discipline. If he can't cut it in pre-school, how is he going to succeed in nursery school?"

"Ernest, our son is trying to tell us something, and you are not listening."

"It's the 'Terrible Twos,' that's all. One day Tommy will thank us for keeping him on the fast track." He checked the time. "Norma, I've gotta go—I'm running a couple of minutes late."

"You don't understand how upset—"

"Let's discuss it tonight during FamilyTime, okay?"

"Good-bye, Ernest."

"Bye, dear."

After hanging up, he wondered if Tommy's behavior wasn't a product of Norma's own negative attitudes. He made a note to bring this up at FamilyTime.

SLACK'S HIDDEN AGENDA

When he entered the conference room at precisely 10:18, Ernest was pleased to see the entire staff in their seats.

"Good morning, everyone. Ms. Minion, will you read the minute of the last meeting?"

Inhaling very deeply, Ms. Minion proceeded to read aloud a highly condensed summary of what had happened at the last staff gathering. So fast and abridged was her reading that it sounded like the chanting of a Sufi mystic. When she finished, 54 seconds later, three people had gone into trances.

Ernest snapped them out of it with a sharp clap of his hands. "Very good, Ms. Minion," he said. Before he could continue, Ivan Slack entered the room and took a seat.

"Hello, everyone," he said cheerily.

"You're late, Slack," Ernest told him. "Normally, I'd give you a mini-Minute Gripe, but—"

"Save your breath," Slack interrupted. "I've got an announcement to make."

"You know my policy, Mr. Slack," said Ernest. "All meetings must hold to the authorized agenda."

"But I have a hidden agenda," Slack announced, producing a memorandum from his vest pocket.

"Ah ha, just as I suspected!" exclaimed Ernest. "Well, then, let's have it. And make it snappy— this is taking up our MeetTime."

"I can now tell you my mission here," Slack stated, somewhat pompously. "I was retained by the Executive Committee some months ago to reduce costs and cut fat. They're putting the entire organization on a strict diet."

"So that's why they sent you to my office," Ernest declared. "Everyone knows I'm the best waste-watcher in the company."

"That may be true," Slack said, "but there is something missing in your department."

"Nonsense! My program has eliminated internal theft. If anyone steals even a minute I know about it."

"I'm not talking about minutes, Ernest. And I'm not talking about paper clips. I'm referring to creativity, warmth, spontaneity—those inefficient human touches that have no place in your operation."

"What are you talking about? My people love their jobs! Right?" Ernest glanced sharply around the conference table as heads nodded quickly up and down. "And there's no fat in my operation. Hell, the way I've got them running, they don't even need aerobics after work!"

"Yes, they work amazingly well," admitted Slack. "My secret survey confirms almost everything you said. But I did find one major area of waste."

"Impossible!" exclaimed Ernest.

"I'm afraid not, Ernest. There's no denying you've conditioned everyone very well with your One Minute Mania. Their discipline is remarkable. You've delegated your duties so efficiently that your operation virtually runs itself."

"You bet it does!" Ernest said proudly.

"In fact, my analysis revealed that your position can now be eliminated. The Executive Committee has decided you're no longer needed. Ernest, you're through."

"What? Impossible! This is the kind of warped humor I'd expect from you, Slack, but enough is enough." Ernest could barely control his anger at the man's impudence. "You're a loose cannon on the corporate deck, and you should be fired."

"It's no joke," Slack replied evenly. "There'll be a formal announcement this afternoon. I thought the staff would want to know as soon as possible. This means no more One Minute Mania."

The first tentative claps quickly gave way to sustained applause, whoops, and whistles from the staff, to Ernest's astonishment. He struggled in vain to regain control of the meeting, shouting, "Next item, please. We're behind schedule!" Finally he stormed out of the room and back to his office.

He felt drained and confused. There had to be some mistake. Ernest called a member of the Executive Committee, a senior vice president known for his kindly, dignified manner.

"Oh, it's you," said the man. "Are you still hanging around?"

"Then it's true!" exclaimed Ernest. "Why was this just sprung on me, with no notice or discussion, not even a grace period?"

"Ernest, haven't you always said grace periods are a disgrace? The Committee chose the most efficient method. We thought you'd appreciate that."

"But I'm the hottest manager in the company. My operation runs like clockwork!"

"True. Unfortunately, the Committee feels you've violated certain sacred principles."

"They're questioning my ethics?"

"It's more serious than that. As you must know, the Peter Principle holds that employees rise to their level of incompetence. It's a law of corporate dynamics."

"That's silly!"

"Oh no, its truth is more profound than your One Minute Mania. The Peter Principle is proven every day across this great land of ours, Ernest. You've violated it by rising to a level of excessive competence."

"But I thought—"

"You've also broken Parkinson's Law—that work expands to fill the available time. You are tampering with the very nature of American business. One Minute Mania is unnatural—it's un-American!"

"But what about productivity and efficiency?"

"Young man, this country is not Japan, thank God. Some other company may welcome your approach—at least for a while. But you've managed your way out of a job here."

"The Committee is making a bad mistake! The Maniac says that—"

"I wouldn't expect you to understand, Ernest. You're the kind of guy who would use a steam shovel to dig his own grave. Good luck and goodbye."

The phone went dead. Ernest felt an unfamiliar feeling of panic rise in his chest. On reflex, he checked his Minute Planner. The precision of his tightly organized schedule usually reassured him. Now it only mocked him with its sudden irrelevance. He'd scheduled a meeting with himself at 3:37 that afternoon. Swallowing hard, he moved it up to the minute at hand.

TERMINAL EMPATHY

Ernest stopped as he was about to call Ms. Minion to tell her to intercept his calls. What calls? What Ms. Minion? His mind was a vortex of confusion. When his phone shrilled its siren call, he almost fell out of his chair before answering it. It was Dr. Clockenspiel, the company's Director of Employee Empathy.

"Ernest, I know this must be a difficult time for you. I'd like to suggest an interface session to make this developing life transition easier. Or are you too busy to see me now?" Dr. Clockenspiel allowed himself a guffaw at this.

"No, I'd like to speak with you. I'll be right down."

When Ernest entered Doctor Clockenspiel's wood-panelled office, he found a distinguished-looking man with an uncanny resemblance to Sigmund Freud. After a rather mechanical handshake, the doctor waved him to a comfortable armchair.

"Ernest, I want to express my deepest empathy. This must have come as quite a shock."

"You're right about that, doctor. It's not only been a major career blow, it's thrown off my schedule for the rest of the day."

"Of course. I want you to know, Ernest, that I'm here to help you come to terms with this event—something I do all the time, for all our employees. Just this morning, I led an encounter session with a group of our smart worker robots."

"You counsel robots?" Ernest asked, amazed.

"Robots are people, too, you know," Dr. Clockenspiel replied sharply. "Your surprise is the kind of thing they are fighting to overcome. This morning's group suffers from severe depression because they're being replaced by even smarter robots. How would you like to spend the rest of your life molding Jell-O in the company cafeteria?"

"That never occurred to me," Ernest admitted. "But doctor, robot depression has nothing to do with my human predicament."

"Oh, but you're wrong. You have made phenomenal career progress here precisely by trying to achieve the superhuman efficiency of robots. It's no problem for robots because human managers don't see them as a threat. But if a human manager begins to seem as efficient as a robot, he or she will be compared to other humans and make them look bad."

"But I'm no threat. My performance only makes my superiors look better."

"You really believe that, don't you? How charming. Didn't the One Minute Maniac warn you this would happen? This chart will explain what I mean. The top line represents optimum robot efficiency. This steep curve shows your remarkable career trajectory. As it approaches the top line it wipes out on this dangerous downward curve."

"What's that?"

"It projects Top Management Backlash. I call it Deadman's Curve. You encountered it today, which is a week later than I'd projected."

"You expected me to be fired?"

"Top managers don't get where they are by letting young hotshots outrun them. I've been tracking your case for quite a while. You're a classic casualty of One Minute Mania."

**Dr. Clockenspiel explains
Top Management Backlash.**

"But why didn't you warn me?" Ernest cried.

"I'm in charge of empathy, not sympathy. Besides, you would have denied it. It goes against your personality."

"And how would you describe my personality, doctor?"

"Like all those who succumb to One Minute Mania, Ernest, you have severe obsessive-compulsive tendencies. You think you can and must impose order on a chaotic world. Since chaos is the natural state of human affairs, your attempts must fail at some point."

"But I'm nowhere near that point. I'm still perfecting my Timastery."

"See what I mean? Timastery is a delusion, Ernest. It's based on a denial of mortality. A subconscious fear of death makes you One Minute Maniacs track time like a miser counts his money."

"That's nonsense."

"You're denying your denial, already?"

"No, I'm not."

"Now you're denying your denial of your denial! Listen to me, Ernest: Everybody has some fear of death."

"Even you, doctor?"

"No, not me. But let's talk about you, Ernest."

"Wait a minute. You just said everyone has some fear of death," Ernest persisted.

"Every person," Doctor Clockenspiel clarified.

"But you're a . . . ."

"I'm not human, Ernest. I'm a robot," the doctor admitted.

"You're a mechanical shrink? I'm baring my soul to a talking vacuum cleaner? This is crazy!" Ernest shouted.

"No, Ernest, everything I told you is true. You must believe me, for your own good."

"No way. I'm getting out of here." Ernest rose and got his coat.

"Ernest, you must abandon One Minute Mania! My charts show...." Doctor Clockenspiel's voice trailed off. Ernest was gone.

THERE'S NO PLACE LIKE HOME

By the time Ernest turned into his driveway, he had regained control. If CanSys was threatened by him, he didn't want to be there anyway. They were too stupid or old-fashioned to see that One Minute Mania was the way of the future. His life was a testimonial to its value.

He made good use of the afternoon, hosing down the rumpus room and programming the new microwave. When Norma came home with Tommy she seemed distant.

"Why are you home, Ernest?" she asked him.

"I was fired. But look," he said quickly, pointing to the microwave, "I added baked Alaska and pigs in a blanket to autocook memory!"

"How nice for you, dear," said Norma. Her voice sounded tight.

"I thought you'd be pleased," Ernest replied proudly.

"I'm leaving you, Ernest. I'm taking Tommy with me."

"What are you talking about?" Ernest couldn't grasp what he'd heard. "If you're upset about anything, Norma, we can discuss it at FamilyTime."

"There's nothing left to discuss. I'm sick of One Minute Mania, I'm tired of living by a stopwatch. I promised to love, honor, and obey, not to sprint nonstop."

"But dear, you can't do this now, when we've accomplished so much," Ernest pleaded.

"I liked you a lot better when you were an underachiever," Norma declared.

"Honey, you can't mean that," Ernest cried. "I've done all this for you and Tommy!"

"You've done it for that Maniac! Tommy and I are not cut out for One Minute Mania, Ernest. Life in the fast lane isn't fast enough for you—you want to *pass* the people in the fast lane! Well, I'm taking this exit." With this, Norma grabbed Tommy by the hand and led him out to their station wagon, as Ernest followed, trying vainly to get her to reconsider.

"I'll be in touch, Ernest. I'd tell you to take it easy, but it would just be a bad joke," Norma said.

"Bye, Daddy."

"Goodbye, son. Don't worry, you and Mommy will be back as soon as she comes to her senses." He gave Tommy a quick hug.

"Don't hold your breath, Ernest," Norma stated. She and Tommy got in the car and drove away.

Ernest sat motionless on the front steps as the evening faded into dusk.

CONFRONTING THE MANIAC

The next day Ernest went to see the One Minute Maniac. He was greeted by Ronnie the Robot. "Hello, Ernest. How nice of you to drop by."

"I have to see the Maniac."

"I'm afraid he's in an important meeting and must not be disturbed."

"But I must speak with him! It's urgent!"

The robot hesitated before speaking. "Very well. Because you are a personal student of the Maniac, you may use the red emergency phone. Here," said Ronnie, handing Ernest the phone. "It's a direct line."

Ernest seized the receiver. "Hello," said the Maniac's voice. "This is the One Minute Maniac speaking. I'm happy to offer you special guidance at this time."

"Maniac!" shouted the distraught young man, "I can't go on! I—" "One Minute Mania is a lifestyle," the voice broke in. "It requires a total commitment if it is to work properly. Please state your problem."

"Maniac!" Ernest repeated, near tears. "My life is in ruins! I think I'm losing my mind. I've gotta see you—I swear it'll only take a minute."

A series of buzzes and beeps came through the receiver. The voice returned. "One Minute Mania is a lifestyle. It requires a total commitment if it is to work properly. I need more information. Please restate your problem."

Suddenly, Ernest realized the truth. "It's a goddamned tape!" he screamed, sending the phone crashing to the floor. "Where is he? I'll kill him!"

As Ernest made for the Maniac's door, the robot moved to block his path. "Unless you leave at once, I will be forced to employ my death ray!"

"Get out of my way, you overgrown coffee pot!" shouted Ernest, shoving the robot into a potted plant. Bursting into the inner office he found the Maniac, dressed in golf clothes and practicing his putting on an antique Persian rug.

"Hello, Ernest. I thought you might come back. Mind stepping aside? You're blocking my putt." The Maniac sent the ball into the center of the cup. The man radiated success and self-assurance in a way that infuriated Ernest now as much as it had beguiled him before.

"I've come to clean your clock," he told the Great One, barely controlling his rage. "You've gone too far—I've lost my job and my family because of One Minute Mania. No one can live by these methods!"

The Maniac put down his putter. "You seem upset, Ernest," he began smoothly. "What's the trouble?"

"You know what the trouble is—you caused it! It's all your fault!"

"Ernest, I just give the public what it wants," he stated calmly. "You know, there's a Maniac born every minute."

"They're not born, they're made—by you. You and your insane ideas!"

"You really believe that, don't you, Ernest?"

"I sure do," replied Ernest. He was finding it difficult to sustain his fury in the Master's presence.

"Ernest, let's examine this situation logically, shall we? Now, when you came to me, you wanted more than anything to end your ineffective, time-wasting ways. You wanted success in your career more than anything else in the world, didn't you?"

"Well, yes, but—"

"And that came to pass, didn't it?" The Maniac's gaze was unrelenting.

"Sure, but I never—"

"Well, what's your problem?"

"I lost my job!"

"You can get another. I've made you a very valuable commodity. There are a hundred companies that would snap you up."

"My wife has left me."

"She'll be back. If not, there are plenty of women who would go for a successful manager like you."

"But I'm not happy."

With chilling speed, all traces of empathy vanished from the Master's face. "HAPPY?" he shouted. *"You never said anything about happiness!"*

This was too much for his listener. Ernest broke down, sobbing convulsively. The Maniac approached him and put both hands on his shaking shoulders.

"Don't you see?" asked the Maniac. "If you wanted happiness, you never really needed me. You had what you needed all along—the brains, the heart, the courage to live your life without a quick fix. Instead, you fell for One Minute Mania. I am shocked to realize it has destroyed your life."

"You are?" said Ernest, wiping his eyes.

"Of course. I never meant you harm."

"Then you'll stop writing these books?"

"Are you crazy?" snorted the Maniac. "I've got ideas for a dozen more! Let me tell you about them—you got a minute?"

With a tortured cry, Ernest vaulted across the desk and lunged for the One Minute Maniac. He was restrained by security guards before he could do serious harm, and swiftly removed from One Maniac Plaza, never to return.

Epilogue

Ernest Fellow's story ends nobly and, indeed, happily. Norma and Tommy returned home after he promised to forget about efficiency. Ernest went on to become a therapist for other One Minute victims, in a clinic without clocks.

The Maniac remains at large.

About the Authors

Jeffrey Book has worked as an editor at Architectural Digest, Rosebud Books, The Knapp Press, and Alfred van der Marck Editions. In addition to his writing, he is much in demand as a mismanagement consultant. Based in Los Angeles, Mr. Book has saved so much time that he loans it to needy friends.

Garrett Soden is art director at Occidental College in Los Angeles. He is also a freelance writer, designer, and composer. With his many pursuits, Mr. Soden leads the lives of three normal people, all of whom resent it. In less manic moments he enjoys a pleasantly inefficient life in Pasadena with his wife, daughter, and Richard the Cat.